POWER

A

98 A

5

WITHDRAWN

For Paul Lowenberg

POWER
Creating it Using it

HELGA DRUMMOND

KOGAN
PAGE

Disclaimer

The masculine pronoun has been used throughout this book. This stems from a desire to avoid ugly and cumbersome language, and no discrimination, prejudice or bias is intended.

Kogan Page Limited
120 Pentonville Road
London N1 9JN

© Helga Drummond, 1991
Reprinted 1993

British Library Cataloguing in Publication Data
A CIP record for this book is available from the British Library.

ISBN 0 7494 0357 8

Typeset by BookEns Ltd, Baldock, Herts.
Printed in Great Britain by Ipswich Book Co. Ltd., Ipswich, Suffolk

Contents

Preface

Ask almost any manager what he most lacks and the answer will be 'power'. By power is meant being able to get things done through being able to procure the right resources, being clear about what is expected, knowing what authority exists, and so on. The last thing that anyone is likely to mention is seeking power for its own sake.

Powerlessness is a major source of managerial inefficiency, resulting in wasted time, needless conflict, stress, anger and frustration. The purpose of this book is to help managers acquire the power they need to do their jobs. The emphasis is upon

power to do,

ie changing relationships with the world through a combination of:

1. Awareness.

2. Resources.

3. Energy.

Awareness centres upon understanding the nature of power; how power relations operate, change, and can be changed. It is emphasized that the necessary resources are everywhere. Dress, language and even gestures can be used to make power. Although energy exists within the self, it is hoped, by supplying two parts of the equation, to stimulate the third. Achievement, after all, depends critically upon:

believing you can win.

This book explains just how easy it can be to succeed.

Power, it is acknowledged, can be used for good or for ill; for personal as well as organizational aggrandisement. It is argued elsewhere in this book, however, that more harm is committed by the powerless, than by those who feel in control of events.

Since almost every human interchange is a power relation, it is envisaged that this book will prove useful in everyday life, as well as at work. The ideas and advice contained in the various chapters do work.

Power relations, however, are inherently unstable, as both sides must grapple with incomplete information about one another, their behaviours influenced by unknown and unfathomable fears, ambitions and jealousies. No guarantee can therefore be given that every power ploy will succeed every time. That said:

I am confident that purchase of this book will prove self-financing.

If it facilitates just one promotion, or enables the reader to save a hundred pounds on a car deal, it will have more than repaid its owner the cover price. I am optimistic that reading and occasionally re-reading what I have to say will yield reward upon reward.

Acknowledgements

This book grew from a Ph.D thesis. I wish to thank my research supervisors, Chris Allinson and Terry Moreton of Leeds University for their enthusiasm and generosity with their time, that most precious of commodities. I am grateful to Bradford City Council who stumped up for the fees, to say nothing of the legendary typing bills. I also wish to thank my former senior colleague Steve Cook for his interest in the research, and Barry Jacobs and Bernard McEvoy for their tuition in the 'street skills' which have enriched this book.

My interest in human energy developed through working with Manchester Business School colleagues Roy Payne, Peter McLavery and Ed Young on an exploratory research project concerned with concepts of hard work and working hard. I am grateful to them for sharing their ideas and knowledge.

Helga Drummond
Liverpool,
July, 1991

Have more than thou showest
Speak less than thou knowest
Lend less than thou owest
Ride more than thou goest
Learn more than thou trowest
Set less than thou throwest
Leave thy drink and thy whore
And keep in a door
And thou shalt have more
Than two tens to a score

Shakespeare, *King Lear*

Introduction

Power concerns:

- getting what you want;
- doing better than you otherwise might.

A basic theme of this book is that desires are often readily attainable. Power is the key to achievement, yet if you wait for someone to give you power, you will wait forever. Nor is it correct to assume that power must be formally conferred, signed, sealed and delivered for it to be real.

Power basically derives from nothing.

Nothing means, quite literally, nothing. Power is created by filling the vacuum of no man's land. As we shall see:

1. Even in the most tightly controlled organizations, some discretion always exists.

2. It is possible to acquire power far in excess of what job descriptions and organization charts might suggest.

While the exercise of power requires resources, it is emphasized that this does not necessarily mean money. This book explains how readily available entities can be used to make power. These include:

1. Dress.

2. Speech.

3. Written communications.

4. Office furnishings.

5. Routine information.

6. Seeing things as other people see them.

7. Questioning assumptions.

8. Time.

9. Energy.

Of these, energy is the most important. Without energy, nothing can be achieved. With energy, anything is possible. Much stress is placed upon initiative. The reader is repeatedly urged not to wait for others to grant permission or to suggest ideas, but to look for power vacuums and fill them. The advice is:

do it.

Once power is created, seldom will anyone take it away. On the contrary, power is self-perpetuating in that:

powerful people are attractive.

and, because they are attractive, they tend to receive more communications, more attention and so on. This generates more power.

Success

Acquiring power is insufficient — it is essential to learn how to use it. Success is the product of:

- vision;
- realism; and
- enjoyment.

Without vision there is nowhere to go. Those who dare to dream create the foundations of their eventual success by projecting themselves into the future. It takes courage to dream, and courage to keep the dream alive.

Enacting a dream requires realism. You cannot go from a hand cart to a Rolls-Royce, at least not in an afternoon. Everyone has to start somewhere. As the Chinese proverb teaches us:

A journey of a thousand miles begins with the first step.

The aspiring pop star, for example, starts by taking a job as a barman in a night-club to bring him closer to where he wants to be. Likewise, the entrepreneur who sells a few novelty ales brewed in his garage is taking the first steps towards the eventual establishment of a PLC.

The people who fail are those who, for whatever reason, never start. The schoolteacher who says to a delinquent pupil, 'For God's sake, do something!' is rendering sound advice. The actions which set people upon the road to achievement are often very simple, perhaps a matter of lifting the telephone, writing a letter or booking an appointment. As a case in point:

- Is there something you have always wanted to do?
- If so, why not start now?

Once an ambition is mobilized, achievement often comes much sooner than was ever imagined possible.

It is always easier to succeed when leading from strength. Strength means doing what you enjoy and are good at. I once asked a company chairman who had started his career from nothing whether he felt he worked hard. 'Work?' he replied, 'This isn't work. Work is getting up at six am twice a week to go into my gymnasium'. If your job is a constant strain, maybe you should think of changing it in favour of something consistent with your talents and aspirations.

Often, in people's lives some critical event occurs which seems to signal something. A trainee lawyer, for example, wins £50 in an essay-writing competition. Might this mean a choice between being a competent solicitor or a brilliant journalist? Recognizing one's true abilities can be disturbing, especially if the choice lies between following a safe if unremarkable path, or a hazardous but potentially highly rewarding one. There are no easy answers. What can be said, however, is that the most potent source of power is that which lies within the self. The individual must decide whether or not to use it.

Fringed with gold

This book stresses the importance of small gains. Small gains are important, because:

contests are often won or lost at the margin.

An Olympic gold medal is decided by a fingertip. The outcome of a horse-race rests on a nose length. Contracts are awarded on the basis of a small price differential. A job offer turns upon one interview question, and so on. Consequently, initiatives such as a little influence exercised here, some goodwill created there, the exploitation of a fragment of information might, just might, prove critical.

Small gains, moreover, often add up to more than the sum of their parts. There are two ways to play the board game of Monopoly. One, known as 'the prince's strategy' is to concentrate upon expensive properties like Mayfair and Park Lane. The alternative, known as 'the pauper's strategy' consists of trading for the cheaper properties such as Old Kent Road and Euston. The emphasis in this book, metaphorically speaking, is upon the latter.

Playing the pauper's strategy in a power context means accepting a little extra responsibility now, a minor promotion later, perhaps securing one or two additional staff, procuring a small increase in budget, and so on. The strength of this approach is that:

small gains are easier to achieve than large ones.

This is not least because no one bothers to oppose isolated and trivial acquisitions. Indeed, such crumbs from the table tend to be scorned by those operating the prince's strategy. Only when the gains have accumulated do they realize what is really happening. By then, of course, it is too late.

Power and daily living and working

Exalted dreams are important, but so is the daily business of life. Here, too, it is possible to do better than objective conditions suggest, by utilizing the ideas and tactics contained in this book. For example, even a simple thing such as thinking through the objectives for a meeting or a visit to the doctor's surgery can make the difference between success and failure. Listening carefully to a salesman or estate agent can save you or your organization substantial sums of money, or from making a bad bargain. Likewise, the manager who takes the initiative by making a short presentation to a meeting is more likely to get what he wants than his counterpart who goes along hoping to 'play things by ear'.

Many of the suggestions contained in this book can be implemented with minimal effort. Just glancing through a file which routinely passes through your hands, for example, can reveal something which one day might be extremely significant. Keeping someone waiting costs nothing, yet it can transform the balance of a power relationship.

Coping with the power of others

The power-seeker's repertoire must equip him to cope with other people's power. This book explains why intuitive responses, such as fighting back when attacked, are often ineffective. One of the paradoxes of power is that choice ultimately rests with the power-target rather than the power-holder. That is, in the last analysis:

no one can force you to do anything.

In extremis, the power-target can choose to die rather than obey. If he does, no matter what resources the power-holder commands, he is thwarted. It is suggested elsewhere in this book that the ultimate source of power is man's fear of death. Hence the Buddhist teaching which stresses 'Don't hold on to', which means, among other things, letting go of personal desires. Letting personal desires go, even including one's life, frees the person from the social and physical constraints that regulate and control the fulfilment of desire. Freedom from desire means not to identify, and so unlocks the person from outside control, thereby enhancing the self as a source of power.

Note on the Questionnaires

These appear twice in each chapter — at the beginning and towards the end. In each case award yourself one point for a correct answer. Naturally, your score should have improved when you have read the chapter and completed the questionnaire for the second time!

1

The nature and dynamics of power

Before reading this chapter, test your understanding by answering the following questions:

1. **The purpose of power is:**
    a) to overcome resistance
    b) to get others to comply
    c) to acquire staff and other resources
    d) to enable you to get what you want.

2. **The best strategy for creating power is to seek:**
    a) absolute control over one thing
    b) tight control over two or three things
    c) tight control over as many things as possible
    d) wide influence and responsibility.

3. **The opportunity arises to expand your power by assuming control of a loss-making department. Do you:**
    a) grasp the opportunity before someone else makes a bid
    b) accept only if you can properly integrate the department within your existing operations and improve its performance
    c) say you will think about it
    d) refuse?

4. **A colleague is seeking control over part of your operations. The staff concerned are an unproductive headache. Do you:**
    a) let him have them
    b) resist

    c)   let him have them but negotiate something in return

    d)   counter-attack by making a bid for his staff?

5. **You are attracted to someone, but he/she seems un-interested. Do you:**

    a)   ask him/her lots of questions about themselves

    b)   talk about yourself

    c)   make small talk

    d)   gossip about other people?

6. **You yearn for the attention of an attractive person, who is surrounded by others all competing for the same. Do you:**

    a)   push your way to the front

    b)   ignore the person

    c)   wait until you can catch the person alone

    d)   create a diversion, which focuses the attention upon you?

7. **Your expertise is required at another location. You manager promises to discuss a salary rise later, provided you move at once. Do you:**

    a)   comply forthwith

    b)   refuse to comply without first obtaining a specific commitment

    c)   comply on the understanding that the review will take place by a certain date

    d)   comply, but ask what sum he has in mind?

8. **Just before the start of a pop concert, the star performer telephones to say he will not turn up unless supplied with a pink Rolls-Royce in order to make an entrance. Do you:**

    a)   find one fast

    b)   send someone else to find one fast

    c)   try and reason with the performer

    d)   tell the performer not to bother?

9. **You have just spent £350,000 on a 'fast' wood-cutting machine. The model supplied works at less than half the required speed. You are due to negotiate with the company representative. What will your opening gambit be?**

    a)   remove the machine

    b)   negotiate a discount

    c)   see what they propose

    d)   cancel the meeting and pass the problem on to your legal department.

10.   **Someone has just taken the credit for your work. Do you:**

    a)   say nothing, but when the chance comes, take secret revenge

    b)   threaten revenge and carry it out

    c)   tell others you will settle the score

    d)   say nothing now but take revenge later, and make sure the other person knows about it?

Power, like love, is impossible to define but easy to recognize.[1] Most of us are familiar with terms like:

- power drive;
- power struggle;
- lust for power;
- the will to power.

Some people devote their lives to the pursuit of power; sometimes the more they strive for power, the more it eludes them. In the popular television series 'Doctor Who', those tin-can terrors known as the Daleks have but one aim in conquering the universe — power.

Why do people want power?

Why do people want power so much? Power can be understood in two ways, namely:

1.   Power over.

2.   Power to do.

Power over someone or something may appear attractive, but after the novelty has worn off, it becomes empty and meaningless, because it is static. What is the point of having power over someone, for example, unless you are actually able to do something with it? As John Fowles' character in *The Collector* discovers, having kidnapped the girl, he has complete power over her, yet paradoxically, he is powerless because he cannot obtain the one thing he wants, ie, for the girl to fall in love with him. Worse, his behaviour has destroyed any possibility of the girl falling in love with him. Force has collapsed in on itself.

Seeking power 'to do' is potentially a much more constructive exercise.

Power prevents society from dissolving into anarchy and impotence. Without the power to protect ourselves from the elements and to obtain food and other essentials, we would not survive long. Power is required to enable us to retain what is rightfully ours. Power is also necessary to accomplish even the simplest tasks. When two men move a piano, for example, one shouts 'Lift!'.[2]

Power in organizations

Organizations require power to produce goods and services. In theory, each member of an organization is allotted sufficient power to enable them to perform effectively — no more and no less. In reality, things are seldom so simple. Managers complain that they lack sufficient power, individuals vie with one another to gain control of staff, information and other resources. Simultaneously, much energy in organizations is devoted to resisting power ploys, and the attempts of the powerful to obtain compliance. Exposure to the whims of the powerful can be an unpleasant experience. Employees are often in fear of others more powerful than themselves.

Fear and power are often correlated. This is partly because 'power to do' often entails 'power over', and because the reality of power depends partly upon the individual's perception. For example, one employee may view a particular supervisor as friendly, whereas another may see him as hostile. Conversely, a supervisor may behave differently towards different people. Some he cajoles, others he coerces, and a few he ignores. These differences are explained by interaction. In interacting, people form images of one another; they react to what they think the other person is feeling and thinking, and may see the other person as more powerful or more sinister than they actually are. These feelings are not evident on any organization chart, but are nonetheless real to those experiencing them.[3, 4]

The ethics of promoting understanding of power

Such are the dark, Machiavellian connotations of power that arguably it is unethical to show people the way to power. I disagree, because:

1. Ruthlessness and savagery often stem from fear.

2. Fear stems from powerlessness, not power.

3. Power actually reduces conflict and violence.

4. Empowered managers are more effective than powerless ones.

A frightened dog is more likely to attack than a confident one. Frightened people are similarly dangerous. They are the ones most prone to lashing out and behaving destructively, because they are afraid: afraid of being blamed, of looking foolish, of being overtaken by others, and so forth. Fear emanates from feelings of powerlessness, ie where the individual feels he cannot control events. Conversely, individuals who feel in command of situations are more likely to use power wisely. They have no need to behave aggressively, to launch into the attack, to destroy others' careers and so on, because they know they have a sense of their own worth and achievements, they know how to get what they want, and that they will get it. Their confidence protects them from excesses. This may explain why SAS soldiers are typically the most quietly-spoken and unassuming of all military personnel.

Powerless managers are ineffective. A research survey carried out with my colleagues at Manchester Business School among senior and middle managers found that *at least* 50 per cent of their working day is wasted because of:

- uncertainty about what they should be doing;
- obstructive trade unions;
- being unable to obtain proper equipment;
- high levels of absenteeism;
- inadequate or non-existent support from senior management.[5]

All of these factors, and many more could be added to the list, are manifestations of powerlessness. Powerlessness results in managers being unable to get things done. Ineffectiveness results in costs to the organization, to say nothing of the stress and frustration experienced by individuals.

Power then is not just about empire-building and personal aggrandisement. It is about enabling managers to do their jobs instead of draining vital productive energy into going round in circles.

The path to power

The purpose of power is to get what you want. Achievement may entail overcoming resistance. Acquiring power, however, is not about encountering resistance for its own sake.[6] Resistance is only addressed if it is unavoidable. Indeed, the basic theme of this book is that:

often, what you want is there for the taking.

As we shall see, it is fear of non-existent resistance and difficulties which creates a self-fulfilling prophecy. The good soldier avoids the battle. Real power can often be obtained with unobtrusive ease. While everyone else is bickering and despairing over what to do, you can be there and back before anyone knows. The first step is to understand the dynamics of power relations. This alone may enable you to get you what you want.

The dynamics of power

To use power, or counter others' power, it is vital to understand that despite appearances:

no power relation is absolute, or one way.

The reasons for this are:

1. The economics of power.

2. The reciprocal nature of power.

3. Countervailing power.

Each of these is now discussed in turn.

The economics of power

All power relations involve a trade-off between the *scope* of power and the *intensity* of power. As figure 1.1 shows:

- the narrower the scope, ie the fewer things controlled, the more intense the power; whereas
- the wider the scope, ie the more things controlled, the less intense the power.[7]

A parent's power over a new-born child is virtually absolute, but limited in scope. A chief executive, on the other hand, responsible for 27,000 staff, has extensive power but only limited control.

The implications of this relationship are:

1. People whose power scope is narrow are vulnerable.

2. Those possessing extensive power seldom know all that is going on.

On the first point, the reader is probably familiar with the phenomenon of the office dragon exercising absolute control over the stock cupboard. The intensity of control may be out of all proportion to the person's

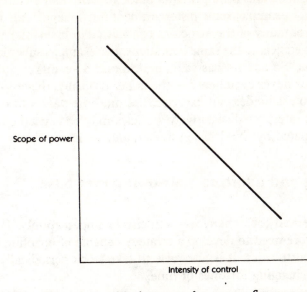

Figure 1.1 The relationship between the scope of power and intensity of control

rank. For example, even the chief executive may have to satisfy this personage that his old biro pen is well and truly spent before being issued with a replacement. Yet if that person's control is removed, their power base is gone — hence their vulnerability.

Narrow, intense power bases are also problematic in the sense that it can be more difficult to control a ship at sea than to govern a nation.[8] A sea captain may have power over his crew, but he is also very exposed, as it is easier for a small crew than for a nation to rebel. Indeed, the Duke of Wellington is reputed to have said of his troops, 'I don't know if they frighten the enemy, but my God, they frighten me.'

As regards the second point, those in seemingly powerful positions are often less powerful than they appear, because they cannot possibly know everything that is going on. So, for example, when a subordinate tells his manager that he has carried out his instructions, how does the manager know that he is speaking the truth? The manager probably has no time to check, and may not know where to look. Even if he were able to enquire, he might still be deceived. For instance, he can be shown a copy letter, but how can he know for certain that the original was ever despatched? He can check whether it has arrived, of course, but then his subordinate can claim it must have been lost in the post.

Those controlling large numbers of people cannot possibly be aware of all the decisions and arrangements made in their name. This may explain why, for example, some historians continue to argue that Hitler was unaware of many of the atrocities committed in his name. Managerial power is subject to the same limitations. For example, subordinates tell others that 'So and So has said', or, 'So and So wants . . .', when 'So and So' has never even heard of the issue. Basically, the less direct control the power-holder can exercise, the more he passes to others. Decisions are interpreted selectively; policies may be carried out in a way unanticipated by the decision maker, and so on.

Developing and auditing your own power base

Organizations and jobs change — sometimes imperceptibly. Power-seekers therefore need to develop a strategy capable of enabling them to exploit opportunities. It is also wise to take stock periodically, and adjust to the changing fortunes of time.

How secure is your power base?

Try and avoid dependence upon one thing or one person as a source of power. The dangers of dependence are illustrated by the tale of the junior manager (A), hungry for promotion, who conspired with his senior (B) to have the head of the organization (C) removed. A's scheme was that once C was ousted, he would obtain B's position, as B would then occupy the job formerly held by C. B nurtured this belief and gave A every encouragement to proceed with his scheme, but otherwise remained in the background.

During the succeeding five years, two things happened. First, A's colleagues, seeing the collusion between A and B, reckoned that their own chances of promotion to B's post were slight. This prompted them to seek advancement elsewhere, and all were successful. Second, when C finally was removed, although B duly succeeded C, B then saw fit to abolish his former post. B, who well understood the art of king-making, determined not to allow A the chance to usurp him. A was therefore left with nothing more than a tarnished reputation and five years of lost opportunity. Instead of learning from this experience, however, A then clung to the hope of succeeding C when the latter retired. A's claim to the post was based upon his seniority. However, in the five further years which elapsed before C retired, junior staff caught up with A. Moreover, his attempts to undermine C during this period only added to his reputation for treachery. When the top post eventually fell vacant, someone else was appointed to it.

A's mistake had been to assume that power must be obtained by design. He would have been better to have retained as many options open as possible by applying for other jobs, and broadening his own power base. The most effective way to extend a power base is not to engage in conspiracy, but to operate unobtrusively by taking on and developing one or two extra responsibilites, cultivating contacts in other departments, widening your experience, and so forth. Such small, easy-to-implement actions add to power through increased responsibility. Moreover, the additional experience gained enhances the power-seeker's career prospects.

Is more necessarily better?

A huge empire is a pleasant thing to survey, but it is potentially counter-productive if it:

- impedes effectiveness;
- raises expectations which cannot be fulfilled;
- stimulates jealousy.

Many people make the mistake of becoming obsessed with acquiring and retaining resources, for their own sake. Power must be organized and skilfully deployed if it is to achieve anything. Might alone is insufficient, and potentially counter-productive. The Americans discovered this in Vietnam; their huge army was rendered helpless and demoralized by ambush attacks, as the Vietcong turned their weakness of inferior numbers into a strength. Like the proverbial cat that choked itself with cream, many managers are undone by gorging upon the artefacts of power. Huge staff numbers are only conducive to achievement if they are necessary, ie fully and gainfully employed. If this is not possible, let go. There is no point in escaping from a sinking ship with pockets full of looted goods, only to be drowned by their sheer weight. Likewise, expansion only makes sense if properly prepared and implemented. If you double your staff or your budget, for example, you will be expected to produce results, and quickly. As with buying furniture, it is a mistake to seize everything and work out what to do with it later.

It is unwise to demand resources every time you are asked to do something. Which manager are you more impressed with: the one who promises to deliver the sun, the moon and the stars if only you will double his staff and his budget in advance, or the one who quietly gets on with the job? Power-seekers are advised to avoid wasting time and energy in hopeless bids and declamations. Instead, they should take the opportunity to show what they can do with what they have. To them, shall more be given.

Avoid appearing clever or successful. This only stimulates fear and jealousy. Although envy is to some extent unavoidable, sagacious managers refrain from provoking destructive emotions unnecessarily. They travel light and humbly, taking only what they need, concealing their gold beneath a beggar's mantle.

Reciprocity: why all leaders are also led

A further reason why control is never absolute is that in power relations:

the power-holder and the power-target are actually influencing one another.

This interaction is known as reciprocity.[9] The implications of reciprocity are important and wide-ranging. Basically, reciprocity explains why:

- power relations are never one way, despite appearances;
- why power relations change over time.

Reciprocity, moreover, can enable the weaker party:

- to equalize the balance of power; or
- even to reverse it.

Why things are rarely what they seem

In power relations, surface appearances are partial. A tiny baby, for example, is utterly dependent upon its parents. Ostensibly then, the parents have absolute control. In reality, the baby controls the parents. When it cries they must attend to it. Their social life, choice of holiday, and so forth are all dictated by it.

Similarly, suicidal people who telephone crisis organizations for help appear to be the needy party. Yet the helper typically needs the client as much as the client needs them. Helpers need to be needed, otherwise they would not be doing the job. Moreover, they too may be suffering from loneliness and depression and have volunteered their services as a means of sustaining themselves.

In organizations, in theory, the manager controls his staff. In reality, the relationship is more complex, as each party influences the other. Many managers perceive an obligation to work longer hours than their staff; their role requires them to set an example over timekeeping, adherence to rules and so forth. The manager must respond to his staff's ideas and problems, often regardless of his own comfort or convenience. As one executive put it, 'Yes, I have power, and power has me.'

How to make someone fall in love with you

Reciprocity explains why hostages frequently develop deep bonds with their captors. The mere presence of another person results in an exchange of influence, even if no one speaks. For example, as the terrorist holds a gun to the victim's head, he notices him, is influenced by his expression, his eyes and so on. Gradually he forms images of him, begins to wonder about his family background and so on. As time progresses, it becomes harder to pull the trigger.

Change occurs faster and more dramatically if conversation ensues. The kidnapper explains his standpoint, and so influences his hostage. The mere fact that the kidnapper senses he has moved the hostage, diminishes his aggression. Identification and attachment deepen when the hostage responds. The interest of both parties is aroused as each perceives it has impressed the other. Reciprocity may also explain why counsellors and therapists sometimes become unprofessionally involved with their clients.

The point is, reciprocity can be used to acquire power. The surest and simplest technique of seduction is to ask the other person questions about themselves. Be patient, as interest develops exponentially, ie:

1. The first time they are surprised.

2. The second time they are expecting it.

3. By the third occasion, they are looking forward to it.

This technique derives its power from the fact that the world is a lonely place. No one really cares about any one else, and people are naturally attracted to those who show a personal interest in them. They also want more of this very pleasant attention. Give it, and before long, they will be coming to you.

The most susceptible are the shy and the diffident. Since they generally perceive themselves as unattractive and/or uninteresting, they tend to be quiet and are therefore deprived of attention. Consequently, when someone shows an interest they are flattered, and respond accordingly. Be careful, however — just as the other person is drawn to you, the likelihood is that you too will enjoy the response and so become more deeply involved.

Penetrating the icon

Engaging reciprocity works even with the most powerful. They too are human, sometimes bored, often anxious. They too quarrel with their partner and worry about their children. However, they may resist or dislike those who are overly familiar. It is therefore best to begin slowly and cautiously, with simple non-contentious questions such as:

- Did you have a pleasant holiday?
- How did the meeting go?
- Are you pleased with your new car?
- How did your son/daughter do in the exams?
- How is your son/daughter settling down at college/university/work?
- How does it feel to be a father/mother?
- Are you going away/doing anything special this year?
- Are you looking forward to Christmas?
- How was the trip?
- How are your chrysanthemums/hens/bees/stamps/coins/grand-children/dogs/etc?

This technique can create valuable bonds and a fund of goodwill, so practise it widely. The final question is universally applicable — everyone has some burning concern or interest, be it their double glazing, their cat breeding prizes, whatever. Find out what it is, and enquire about it sincerely and unhurriedly every time you meet.

Flattery is another way of engaging reciprocity. The most effective form of flattery is that which confirms the other person's image of themselves. For example, someone who prides himself on his leadership skills will be moved by remarks such as, 'This place has certainly sharpened up since you arrive,' or, 'Before, we were just drifting; we feel we know where we are going now and it's helping us stand up to other departments.' The risk with flattery which is at variance with the other person's perceptions is that they may see through it. Even then, they still like it and can soon persuade themselves that it's true. Follow Disraeli's advice and lay it on with a trowel.

How to capture the attention of someone surrounded by admirers

The answer is, ignore them. The other person will notice you because

you are different, and, he will be puzzled as to why you are not interested in him. For those reasons, he will want your attention and, as
they say, be right over.[10]

A variation of this tactic can be used to gain attention in meetings. If
everyone is talking at once, the best way to be heard may be to sit
silent. Others will eventually become curious, anxious even to know
what you think. They may be worried that they have made fools of
themselves or that you know something they do not. Hold out a little
and they will almost beg you to speak, and, when you do, an attentive
audience is assured.

An arranged marriage

Reciprocity can be effected via a third party. Marriage brokers are said
to have practised this technique in order to smooth arrangements: the
method is for the third party to tell the woman that the man, whom
she has never met, finds her attractive. This immediately arouses her
interest. The man receives the same information. His interest too is
aroused. When the two people eventually meet, both are intrigued and
well disposed to one another.[11]

Paying someone a compliment via a third party has a similar effect.
It is highly probable that it will reach the recipient, as people generally
like to transmit good news. The technique can, for example, be used to
help obtain employment. Making it known that you are impressed
with the other person's organization, their managerial ability and so
forth is a potentially powerful means of paving the way to success.

Bear in mind, however, that these ideas can work in reverse.
Enemies may use them to turn others against you. There is little that
can be done to prevent this. The best advice is:

1. Always take the opportunity to ingratiate yourself.

2. Always explore the other person's perceptions of you, particularly
   if you sense they have suddenly become negative.

3. Listen to what others tell you, but never believe them.

Reciprocity and dependence

Power relations are based upon dependence. Dependence may be
uneven but it is never completely asymmetrical. For example,
although an employee may be highly dependent upon his manager for
his job and for promotion, the manager is dependent upon the

employee's skill, energy and integrity, all of which reflect upon him. The point is:

> *however weak the other party may be, he invariably has*
> *some power.*

It is not the amount of power that is important, but how it is used. In self-defence classes, for example, participants are taught techniques which enable the frailest of individuals to overcome an aggressor. It is possible to escape from a stranglehold by turning one's head and so loosening the attacker's grip. Likewise, pressing on a pressure point can achieve the same effect.

Who needs who?

Applying this idea to organizations, power subjects can discover their own strength, for example, by asking:

> *who needs who?*

For example:

1. If I do not do this, who else can or will?

2. If I withhold this, where else could the other person go for it?

3. How much does the other person need my custom/support?

4. What are the consequences for the other person if I do not do this?

Beware of overestimating your own importance. The graveyards are full of people considered indispensible. Although this analysis may reveal how *little* the other party needs you, that in itself is a source of strength, as it facilitates a realistic assessment of the possibilities.

Power is not about conquering the world, but about achieving a better outcome than might otherwise be possible. The key point to remember is:

> *pursuit of the unattainable means forgoing the possible.*

The drunk who looks for his car keys, not where he dropped them but where the light happens to be good, is pursuing the unattainable, and simultaneously rendering the attainable impossible.[12]

For example, employees who try to create consternation and embarrassment by staging a dramatic walk-out usually discover they have had as much impact upon the organization as a hawthorn on a combat jacket. Furthermore, however just their cause, they then find themselves fighting from the outside, without a job, and with the prospect of explaining their behaviour to prospective employers.

A far wiser strategy is to recognize reality, ie that the boss probably wants rid of you too, and may therefore be willing to agree reasonable severance terms. Walking out in pursuit of an unattainable objective, on the other hand, deprives the employee of what he might have had.

It is equally important not to underestimate your power. When Rupert Murdoch wanted to sack Harold Evans, the former editor of *The Times*, Evans recognized that Murdoch had no legitimate reason for dismissal and therefore needed Evans to co-operate by resigning. Evans states that he came under enormous pressure to resign, on the understanding that his pension and other benefits would be arranged later. Evans, however, recognized:

the best time to negotiate is when the other party needs you.

While ever Evans was in his post, Murdoch needed to negotiate. Evans also recognized that once out of office he would be dependent upon Murdoch's goodwill. He did not in fact resign until the severance terms had been agreed.[13]

Who now needs who?

Dependency alters over time, and therefore it is important to be alert to the signs of change in a relationship. As the other party becomes stronger it is essential to recognize the fact, and accommodate them accordingly. Resistance, on the other hand, provokes rebellion. Here is how the old Queen Elizabeth I kept her throne and her head:

> When the session of parliament began, it was found that there was great and general discontent on the subject of monopolies. These grants to private persons of the sole right to sell various articles had been growing in number, and were felt to be oppressive. . . . The monopolies . . . were Elizabeth's frugal method of rewarding her favourites or officials; and to protest against them amounted to an indirect attack on the royal prerogative. Elizabeth had not been accustomed to put up with interferences of this kind from the Commons; how often, for less cause than this, had she railed them in high displeasure, and dismissed them cowering from her presence! And so no one was surprised when she sent for the Speaker, and the poor man prepared himself for a tremendous wigging. Great was his amazement. She greeted him with the highest affability; told him that she had lately become aware that

'divers patents, which she had granted, were grievous to her subjects,' . . . and promised immediate reform. The Speaker
departed in raptures. With her supreme instinct for facts, she had
perceived that the debate . . . represented a feeling in the country
with which it would be unwise to come into conflict; she saw that
policy dictated a withdrawal; and she determined to make the
very best use of an unfortunate circumstance.

(Strachey, L (1971) *Elizabeth and Essex*,
Penguin, Harmondsworth, pp. 175–6)

Countervailing power

One of the laws of power is that:

the exercise of force always results in a counter-force.[14]

Countervailing force is a direct form of reciprocation. It is the factor
which restrains power-holders from behaving in a tyrannical or
capricious fashion. For example, an employee who is unfairly treated
by his manager can counter via the grievance procedure.

Countervailing power can take some peculiar forms. An office
junior, for instance, was continually bullied and derided by his manager.
Whenever the manager was out, the junior countered by pouring salt
from the salt cellar which the manager kept on his bookcase for his
lunch-time sandwich on to the carpet. While not a devastating
response, it was nevertheless eloquent, to say nothing of what it cost
the manager in salt!

The weaker party's ability to counter may succeed in thwarting
totally the stronger party's objectives. The manager referred to in the
previous paragraph arbitrarily decided to extend his share of space in
the open-plan office, by moving his filing cabinets outward by a metre.
The staff felt this was grossly unfair, but were afraid to protest openly.
Instead, every day, they moved his cabinets back a centimetre or two,
until the manager ended up with less space than he had had in the first
place, without him ever realizing it!

Strategies for countering force

The alternatives are either:

- to meet force with force; or
- to counter with a different form of power.

It is said, for example, that the rise of Hitler required the strong personality of Churchill to oppose him. Conversely, Ghandi successfully countered the British not by armed warfare, which would have been disastrous, but by passive resistance.[15] Countering with a different form of power often seems a risky or even foolhardy option, but it can be surprisingly effective. For instance, you can grapple with a mad dog — or lie down, and pretend to be dead. Counter-intuitive tactics may be the only option where the power-holder is extremely strong. These are discussed further in chapter four.

Revenge

Countervailing power can take the form of outright revenge. A Chinese proverb, however, states that if you plan revenge, dig two graves — one for your victim and one for yourself. Revenge is dangerous, because it is destructive. Emily Brontë's character, Heathcliffe, exacts a terrible vengeance against those who had hurt him as a down-and-out youth, but destroys the one he loves, and therefore himself, in the process.

Another reason revenge is dangerous is that its very sweetness tempts perpetrators to flaunt their triumphs. To humiliate someone is to make a dangerous enemy, especially if the humiliation is public. Never deceive yourself into believing that you are safe because the other person is too weak to reciprocate. Ice thaws, and you may be providing the very impetus for that person to change. History is rich in examples of people who have devoted their entire lives to avenging real or imaginary wrongs. The wheel is forever in spin — sooner or later, your deeds will be visited upon you.

This is not the place to discuss the ethics of revenge. If you must exercise vengeance, then follow the tried and tested precept of the Mafia, ie:

silence.

Members of the Mafia never betray anger if someone transgresses against them. Instead, they secretly avow revenge, and ensure that the victim never even suspects that someone has acted against him.

An army private, for example, ridiculed by his sergeant, secretly decided to obtain revenge. One of the sergeant's duties was to punch computer cards (this is an old story), a task at which he was less than competent. The private surreptitiously repunched the cards and so the entire army payroll was thrown into chaos. The sergeant was not only censured for the mistake, but his superiors lost all confidence in him when he was unable to account for how it had happened.

The private was promoted to sergeant following the unceremonious departure of his superior. He later developed a secret hatred towards one of his own troops, who had flirted with his wife. He therefore resolved to ruin him. One of the trooper's duties was to ensure that all the camp windows were secured. One night, after the task had been completed, the sergeant covertly reopened them all. The sergeant then carried out his normal inspection and 'discovered' this serious breach of discipline.

As the reader will have realized, for all his deviousness, the sergeant nevertheless made the mistake of telling someone what he had done. Few people can resist showing off their cleverness, and it usually undoes them.

Avoid creating enmity

One of the corrupting effects of power is that it can lead to managers viewing subordinates as objects of manipulation.[16, 17] A brash statement or gesture, instantly forgotten by the manager, may rankle for years with the employee. Be mindful therefore of the adage about not kicking people on the way up, as you might meet them coming down. Treat others as you would wish to be treated, and, before behaving negatively towards an employee, imagine him ten years from now as your boss.

Summary

- Power is difficult to define but easy to recognize.

- Power can be understood as consisting of power over, and power to do.

- Power is required to accomplish even the simplest task.

- The powerless are potentially more dangerous than the powerful.

- Powerlessness and organizational ineffectiveness are correlated.

- Power is about getting what you want.

- Resistance is by no means inevitable in power relations. What you want may well be there for the taking.

- Despite appearances, power relations are never absolute, or one-way.

- All power relations involve a trade-off between scope and intensity.

- Those possessing narrow power bases are vulnerable.

- Those possessing wide power bases seldom know all that is going on.

- It is advisable to create as wide a power base as possible, eg by assuming extra responsibility.

- Avoid being greedy. Take only what you need and can deploy properly.

- All power relations are reciprocal, ie both parties are actually influencing one another.

- Sometimes it is the seemingly weaker party who is actually in control.

- An excellent way of arousing another person's interest is to ask them questions about themselves.

- If, however, the other person is surrounded by attention, ignore them.

- Reciprocity can be engendered via a third party, eg if you pay someone a compliment, it generally gets back to them.

- Power relations change over time. It pays to reassess the balance of power relations periodically, and adjust accordingly.

- Pursuit of the unattainable obviates the attainable.

- Force is always met by countervailing force.

- It can be extremely effective to counter with a different form of power.

- If you must exercise revenge, do it secretly.

- Before behaving negatively towards a subordinate, imagine him ten years from now as your boss.

UNDERSTANDING POWER QUESTIONNAIRE

Having read the chapter, answer the questions again:

1. **The purpose of power is:**

    a) to overcome resistance
    b) to get others to comply
    c) to acquire staff and other resources
    d) to enable you to get what you want.

2. **The best strategy for creating power is to seek:**

    a) absolute control over one thing
    b) tight control over two or three things
    c) tight control over as many things as possible
    d) wide influence and responsibility.

3. **The opportunity arises to expand your power by assuming control of a loss-making department. Do you:**

    a) grasp the opportunity before someone else makes a bid
    b) accept only if you can properly integrate the department within your existing operations and improve its performance
    c) say you will think about it
    d) refuse?

4. **A colleague is seeking control over part of your operations. The staff concerned are an unproductive headache. Do you?**

    a) let him have them
    b) resist
    c) let him have them but negotiate something in return
    d) counter-attack by making a bid for his staff?

5. **You are attracted to someone, but he/she seems uninterested. Do you:**

    a) ask him/her lots of questions about themselves
    b) talk about yourself
    c) make small talk
    d) gossip about other people?

6. **You yearn for the attention of an attractive person, who is surrounded by others all competing for the same. Do you:**

a) push your way to the front
b) ignore the person
c) wait until you can catch the person alone
d) create a diversion which focuses the attention upon you?

7. **Your expertise is required at another location. Your manager promises to discuss a salary rise later, provided you move at once. Do you:**

a) comply forthwith
b) refuse to comply without first obtaining a specific commitment
c) comply on the understanding that the review will take place by a certain date
d) comply but ask what sum he has in mind?

8. **Just before the start of a pop concert, the star performer telephones to say he will not turn up unless supplied with a pink Rolls-Royce in order to make an entrance. Do you:**

a) find one fast
b) send someone else to find one fast
c) try and reason with the performer
d) tell the performer not to bother?

9. **You have just spent £350,000 on a 'fast' wood-cutting machine. The model supplied works at less than half the required speed. You are due to negotiate with the company representative. What will your opening gambit be?**

a) remove the machine
b) negotiate a discount
c) see what they propose
d) cancel the meeting and pass the problem on to your legal department.

10. **Someone has just taken the credit for your work. Do you:**

a) say nothing, but when the chance comes, take secret revenge
b) threaten revenge and carry it out
c) tell others you will settle the score
d) say nothing now but take revenge later, and make sure the other person knows about it?

Answers overleaf.

Answers to questionnaire

1. **d.**

2. **d** — control may be loose, but this is compensated for by an extensive scope of power, and wide influence.

3. **b** — you should have seen this coming a long time ago and have assessed whether it is an opportunity or a crown of thorns.

4. **c** — never give something away, even if you want rid of it, if you can possibly get something for it. D is the best response if you want to keep the staff, as it provides a distraction.

5. **a.**

6. **b.**

7. **b** — obtain a commitment while your boss needs you. Ignore arguments about it delaying things; he is the only one creating delay.

8. **d** — it sounds risky, but it will work. Besides where are you going to get a pink Rolls-Royce from at this time of night?

9. **a** — this is the last thing the other side wants. It will force them to propose a more generous discount than they probably had in mind. C only hands them the initiative.

10. **a.**

Score before reading chapter ——

Score after reading chapter ——

References

1. Martin, R (1977) *The Sociology of Power*, Routledge & Kegan Paul, London.
2. Wrong, D H (1979) *Power, Its Forms, Bases and Uses*, Basil Blackwell, Oxford.
3. Heider, F (1958) *The Psychology of Interpersonal Relations*, John Wiley, New York.
4. Mitroff, I I 'Why our old pictures of the world do not work any more'. In E E Lawler, M Mohrman, S A Mohrman, G A Ledford and T G Cum-

mings (1985) *Doing Research that is Useful for Theory and Practice*, Jossey-Bass, London.

5. McLaverty, P and Drummond, H (1991) 'The impact of effort in organizations', *Working Paper Series*, Manchester Business School.
6. Hardy, C (1985) 'The nature of unobtrusive power', *Journal of Management Studies*, 22(4), pp. 384–99.
7. Wrong, op. cit.
8. Wrong, op. cit.
9. Simmel, G (1955) *The Sociology of George Simmel* (tr K H Wolff), Free Press, Glencoe, Ill.
10. Watzlawick, P, Weakland, J H, Fisch, R (1974) *Change: Principles of Problem Formation and Resolution*, Norton, New York.
11. Watzlawick et al., op. cit.
12. Watzlawick et al., op. cit.
13. Evans, H (1983) *Good Times: Bad Times*, Weidenfeld & Nicolson, London. London.
14. Galbraith, J K (1984) *The Anatomy of Power*, Hamish Hamilton, London.
15. Galbraith, op. cit.
16. Kipnis, D (1976) *The Powerholders*, University of Chicago Press, Chicago.
17. Kipnis, D (1972) 'Does power corrupt?' *Journal of Personality and Social Psychology*, 24, pp. 33–41.

2

Something can be made from nothing

Test your ability to create power by answering the following questions:

1. **A new employee looks lost and unhappy. Do you:**

    a)   take him under your wing
    b)   take him to the manager
    c)   send him back to the personnel office
    d)   ignore him?

2. **Normal practice is to appoint new staff at the bottom of the salary scale. You wish to appoint above this level. The rule-book says you have 'discretion to vary normal arrangements in exceptional circumstances'. Do you:**

    a)   check with the personnel office what 'exceptional circumstances' means
    b)   ask the personnel office for a ruling
    c)   discuss it with the chief executive
    d)   decide for yourself that the circumstances are exceptional, and offer more than the bottom of the scale?

3. **There has been a serious flood in the building over the weekend; consequently your own office is uninhabitable. There is a vacant office downstairs which you have always coveted. Do you:**

    a)   move in immediately
    b)   wait a day or two and then move in
    c)   ask if you can use the office temporarily
    d)   wait and see what the plans are?

4. **You have been asked to write a short article for a trade journal, which is a good opportunity to get your name publicized. Do you:**
    a) write down whatever comes into your head and send it off
    b) write down whatever comes into your head but then work at it
    c) jot down a few ideas and then do some research
    d) get someone else to research it?

5. **A sales representative from an employment and management consultancy firm seeks an appointment with you. Do you:**
    a) give him half an hour
    b) ask someone else to see him
    c) ask to see a brochure first
    d) decline?

6. **A government agency has enquired about purchasing one of your products. They sound as if they are almost ready to sign a contract which could result in huge orders. Do you:**
    a) tell your boss that all his problems are solved
    b) say nothing to anyone and await developments
    c) tell your boss that some progress has been made and devote all your time to clinching the contract
    d) say nothing, and renew your efforts to secure business elsewhere?

7. **You want to buy a piece of project management software costing £800. Financial regulations state that all orders for non-emergency items must be placed centrally, which takes a long time and often results in endless questioning and argument. Do you:**
    a) get what you need and be prepared to defend your actions later
    b) sit down with a cup of coffee and the rule-book and see if there is a way round the problem
    c) try and obtain an exemption
    d) place an order in the proper way?

8. **You have a choice of how you spend a day. Assuming your objective is to increase power, which option would you select:**

a) go through the budget making sure everything is on target
b) use the opportunity to catch up on outstanding tasks
c) attend a conference
d) 'walk the floor'?

9. **A major contract is due for renewal. Do you:**

a) routinely invite suppliers to tender
b) arrange to meet prospective contractors informally
c) delegate the work but ask to be kept informed
d) delegate the whole thing and forget about it?

10. **Your manager is absent long-term sick with a stress-related illness as a direct result of the problems of managing the department. Do you:**

a) volunteer to deputize at once
b) stand back and let your rival volunteer
c) decide you will deputize if asked
d) wait to see if you are asked and then think about it?

King Lear's declaration, 'Nothing can be made of nothing', suggests he understood little about the nature of nothing.

Nothing is the source of all power.

By 'nothing' is meant space or vacuum; power is created by filling it. The Romans, for example, exploited a potential power vacuum in conquering England, first by invading and then via the establishment of towns, communications, law and order. Likewise, in building a castle at the mouth of a river, power is created through the ability to monitor traffic and receive early warning of potential invaders. When governments topple, the ensuing confusion amounts to a vacuum, and whoever fills it seizes power.

Where to find nothing in organizations

Vacuums abide in no man's land. In organizations, no man's land exists as shown in figure 2.1.

The *permitted* zone represents those things which the organization explicitly allows and/or encourages, such as parking arrangements, holiday entitlements, day release facilities, and so on. The *discretionary* zone represents issues where organizational rules and policies are:

- silent;
- flexible; or
- ambiguous.

No rule-book, for example, can legislate for all the permutations of human behaviour. No conditions of service manual can cover every eventuality. All complex organizations require flexibility — as witness the chaos caused when, for instance, railway staff decide to work to rule.

The *forbidden* zone refers to issues which the organization expressly prohibits, such as outside employment, certain forms of dress, consumption of alcohol on duty, and so on.

The potential for power exists in all three zones. The permitted and the forbidden are basically encapsulated in the organization's authority system, discussed in the following chapter. Attention here focuses upon the discretionary zone and the opportunities it presents to increase power.

The margin of discretion

In theory, everyone in organizations operates within structurally-defined limits. Organization charts, job descriptions, rules and regulations

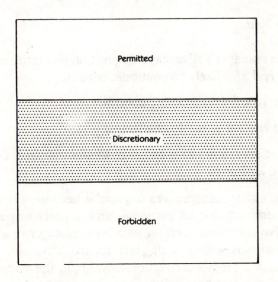

Figure 2.1 The three zones of organizational control

specify the allocation of power. In reality, even in the most tightly-prescribed authority systems, employees always possess a margin of discretion.[1]

Discretion arises because organizations exist on two levels, ie the formal and the informal. The following organization charts represent, respectively:

1. What should be.

2. What is.[2]

The chart in figure 2.2 represents the formal organization. It shows six managers of equal status reporting to a group manager. The chart in figure 2.3 shows the informal organization which operates in reality. The manager responsible for data base systems is more powerful than his colleagues, because his post gives him control over information, and information is essential for decision-making. This makes his colleagues dependent upon him, and gives him greater access to the group manager, who finds the data base manager's services in supplying, interpreting and summarizing information extremely useful. Additionally, the data base manager is temporarily responsible for south area, as the manager there is ill. Furthermore, although theoretically the area managers control their own administrative staff, in practice, these staff take most of their instructions from the data base manager, as only he can provide specialist support and direction.

To have is to hold

The data base manager's advantageous position was unintended, but is nevertheless real and likely to continue, because:

1. Power derives from assuming control.

2. Assumed control is rarely challenged.

3. If assumed control goes unchallenged, eventually it is converted to legitimate authority.

The job of data base manager was unpopular because it is deskbound. Only the incumbent saw its potential, and, equally important, then exploited it. No one authorized the data base manager to assume control of the administrative staff, but having done so, it became extremely difficult for his colleagues to revert to the status quo. Nor did anyone ask the data base manager to cover for the absent colleague. He saw the vacuum, and swiftly filled it. The additional experience

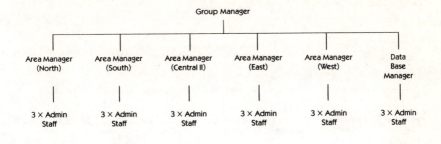

Figure 2.2 The formal organization

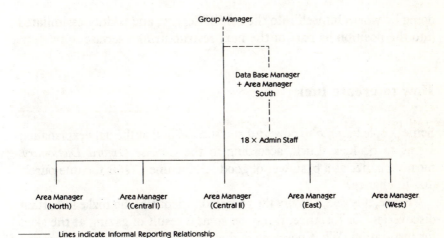

Figure 2.3 The organization as it really operates

further increased his power by widening his knowledge and employment prospects. Knowledge cannot be taken away from him.

Figure 2.4 overleaf shows what will shortly be. The group manager feels strained relating to six people. A vacuum exists, in that there are tasks he should delegate, but he feels it would be unfair to impose such responsibility on the managers. Little by little, however, the data base manager exploits his access to the group manager, using his knowledge and his experience in order to accept additional responsibility. In so

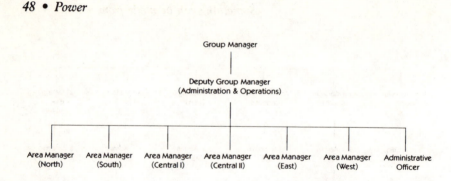

Figure 2.4 The organization as it eventually becomes

doing he works himself into the role of deputy, and is duly assimilated into the position as part of the next restructuring exercise.

How to create luck

Some people become so powerful and successful that the only explanation seems to be luck. Luck, according to the *Concise Oxford Dictionary*, means 'chance as a bestower of good . . . fortune.' Yet is fortune purely due to chance?

Chance, it is said, favours the prepared. Scientists who make important discoveries, for instance, rarely do so as a result of gazing at the skies for inspiration. What happens is that through reading, experimenting and other efforts, ideas are stimulated, possibilities are explored, connections are recognized, and then eureka!

The point is, in many situations,

- the chance may be fortuitous, but,
- the capacity to recognize and exploit it most certainly is not.

Luck can be created by smart work in perceiving what will be needed, and hard work in preparing in readiness for opportunities. For instance, seven years ago, everyone thought a colleague of mine eccentric attending evening classes in Urdu. Today, an increasing number of advertisements for top posts in cities such as Birmingham indicate a preference for candidates fluent in an Asian language.

For those who have only their energy

It is wrong to assume that success depends upon charm, good looks and influential contacts, and to say, 'I have none of these: I never will, therefore I must remain as I am.' Useful though such assets are:

the key to achievement is energy.

Without energy, influence and connections are nothing. Conversely, with energy, everything is possible. Energy is what enables you to change your relationship with the world. The change may be small at first, but small successes lead to bigger ones. Energy is the means whereby individuals can work themselves out of poverty and desolation.

Capitalizing upon energy

The prime focus of most people's energy in organizations is upon their jobs. In every organization there is more to be done than anyone has time to do. This means that most employees, managers especially, can exercise choice over what tasks they perform and how they perform them.[3,4] Even the most tightly supervised employee possesses some freedom, even if it is only to work harder than everyone else. Hard work always gets noticed; power is increased, however, when energy is deployed skilfully. Here are some suggestions:

1. Review what you do.
2. Review how you do it.
3. Be the one who does the work.
4. Accept additional responsibility.
5. Support others.
6. Seize the initiative.

Each of these is now discussed in turn.

Review what you do

Many people do their jobs in a purely reactive fashion. They deal with whatever arises, never recognizing that some aspects of their role are potentially more rewarding than others. They let the job run them, instead of the other way about. Obviously, in any job there are things which *must* be done, but within that constraint, a job can be viewed as a means to an end, the end being power and success.

Before reading any further, try the following exercise:

Self-empowerment exercise

1. List all the tasks you perform regularly.

2. Cross out all except those which you *absolutely* must do. The reader may be astonished to see just how much discretion exists. Now for the next step:

3. List the things you are good at and/or enjoy doing.

4. List all the things you would like to do.

5. Compare these two lists with the first two. The greater the correlation between them, the better the use you are making of your time. If the correlation is weak, then:

6. Write out your role as you would wish to see it.

7. Start doing it.

The purpose of this exercise is to enable power-seekers to identify their potential, and so capitalize upon it by leading from strength. Why sit bored in your office all day, when you could be enjoying yourself at meetings and getting noticed? Conversely, if you enjoy analytical work, why waste time feeling shy and uncomfortable in meetings when you could be studying how to improve say, a production process? A personnel manager, for instance, realized that he spent a disproportionate amount of time on administration, which he disliked and which resulted in him becoming isolated within the organization. He also saw that he spent very little time talking to people, something which he enjoyed. So, the personnel manager delegated some administrative work and began interviewing all new employees after they had spent six months in the organization. This resulted in increased enjoyment and increased power, as the interviews enabled him to discover what was happening in the various departments. Moreover, as a consequence of being interviewed in this way, staff came to regard the personnel manager as having ultimate control, thus further adding to his power. No one had told the personnel manager to do this, but no one stopped him.

The ideal state to aim for is where the job virtually becomes a hobby. That said, many ambitious people are prepared to do work they dislike in order to further their long-term goals. This is obviously a personal choice; power-seekers should note, however, that if the strain involved is heavy and likely to be prolonged, it might be advisable to look for a job where you can shine more easily.

Review how you do it

Many seemingly energetic managers waste more time than they ever use. Although they boast about getting up at five every morning and about working 15-hour days, they often achieve substantially less than those who work a standard day. One reason for such under-achievement is that the energy of such highly-charged people often works against them. That is, being endowed with copious verve, they never ask:

what for?

These workhorses believe that if it's hurting, it must be doing good. So, if they keep themselves and everyone else up until midnight, night after night, they must be doing great things. Such 'machos' initially make a good impression, with their impatient gestures and quick and clean way of wielding pencils. Others, however, soon become dis-enchanted when they see just how much human and other capital these people waste as a result of charging into situations without any forethought or planning.

Another reason that highly dynamic people under-achieve is that their energy leads them to over-estimate their abilities. Consequently they typically initiate dozens of projects. Their list of objectives looks impressive, until they begin to be reiterated year after year, as none are ever completed. Much better to concentrate upon one target and achieve it, than to discredit yourself through being unrealistic.

This does not contradict the point made earlier about the impor-tance of energy. Power-seekers often work extremely hard indeed. The difference between them and the dynamic machos, however, is that power-seekers make haste slowly. They think before they act. They tell themselves that everything they do must be for something. Above all, they know how to use their time.

Powerful time management

Managers tend to view time as a master rather than as a servant. To the majority, time is a source of pressure and stress, as there is never enough of it.[5] Power-seekers think differently. They see time as a resource, and therefore a potential source of power if managed appropriately. Time management is about exploiting the margin of discretion available to gain an edge on others. Competitive edge results from superior efficacy, through:

- getting more done;
- meeting deadlines; and, by no means least,
- better quality work.

There are many excellent books on the subject of time management, and the reader would be well advised to consult some of these. It is stressed, however, that time management alone is insufficient, it must be combined with task management. Basically the aim of such a combined approach is:

whatever you do, make it tell.

Many managers waste hours of their time staring at the wall, chatting away the time of day, half-heartedly starting one task, then another, and finishing none, and so on. They look back at the end of the day and realize they have done nothing. Worse, most of the week is like that.

Thoughtfulness is the key to powerful time and task management, ie before moving into action ask yourself:

1. Why am I doing this?

2. How can I best do it?

3. When can I best do it?

For example, take a simple thing like going through the mail, a task which might take an hour or so. Why are you doing it if you have a secretary? How much do you need to see and how much could the secretary deal with routinely? When the file arrives, do you approach it randomly, or sort it first into urgent, important, and so on? Better still, ask the secretary to do it for you. Do you need to read every report in detail?

Before starting any job, think through what is involved. This prevents time being wasted through vital stages being missed, and may also reveal potential short-cuts. It also reduces the likelihood of becoming stuck half way through a task and having to start again.

The 'when' aspect of time management is the most neglected. Essentially there are two types of time, ie:

- quality time;
- the rest.

Quality time is defined as time when powers of energy and

concentration are highest. It exists as the individual defines it, maybe early in the morning, or when the office is quiet, or on Sunday afternoons. Quality time is the time to enact a powerful performance. Give your quality time to important tasks, and the rest to other jobs. Learn to use odd half-hours to profit, and to minimize unproductive time. For example, why spend two hours unoccupied in a meeting when you can be jotting down a few ideas, or perhaps drafting a letter?

Will is critical to achievement. Plans are useless unless enacted. Instead of bemoaning interruptions, manage them. Set time aside when you may be interrupted, and use it to discharge short-cycle tasks requiring little concentration. No law exists requiring you to pass hours in gossip and conversation. Maintaining good relations with people does not necessitate spending half the day in their company. Above all, never wait until you feel like doing something before starting, otherwise you will never start. The tiredness that often descends before beginning a job often stems from fear of starting. The way to overcome the problem is to start. If motivation is low, tell yourself you will limit the time spent on it. Once started, you will probably find that the work generates its own momentum.

Using time to create power

A further way in which time can be manipulated to create power is through exploiting discretion in order to:

- speed matters up; or
- to delay them.

Speed is a foreign word in many organizations. At the simplest level, many people lose out because they are too slow. Power-seekers never allow themselves to be overtaken by events. If it is necessary to get in first, they do so, and they always deliver.

On another plane, demands for speed can be used to apply pressure, to escape from bad bargains and unwise commitments. Time is manipulable simply by taking the initiative. Instructions such as, 'If it's not here tomorrow, the order is cancelled', and 'I expect to see the report on my desk tomorrow morning', are examples of using time as a lever to coerce the other party. Controlling time in this way involves striking a balance between:

appearing reasonable, while knowing that the other party cannot meet the deadline imposed.

Delaying tactics are another means of controlling time. Delay works best when the other party is ill-equipped to withstand it.[6] The lover who arrives late for an assignation, for example, is using control over time to make the other party anxious, and consequently more appreciative of him. Likewise, a protracted grievance procedure or law suit are means of wearing down the other party's resistance and so thwarting him.

Whereas speed can be used to prevent a person from changing his mind, delay can be invoked to achieve a change of heart. Persuasion works by allowing the other party time to reflect upon and reconsider his position. Inaction too can be used in the power-seeker's favour. Absence, for example, makes the heart grow fonder. Likewise, conflicts often result from unwarranted intervention, which destabilizes a state of affairs — what Watzlawick and his colleagues describe as two people frantically trying to steady a steady boat.[7] Again, this is where the highly energetic types described earlier in this chapter undo themselves. Their first impulse is to act, when often the best course of action is to leave matters alone and let time do its work.

Doing the work

Organizations are full of people who love to attend meetings, sit on committees, and talk. Although these enthusiasts may excel at criticizing others' efforts, while nevertheless taking the credit for their own success, seldom do they actually do anything. Although their idleness is irritating, it nevertheless creates a potentially useful vacuum, because:

- doing the work creates dependency;
- dependency creates power.

Doing the work connected with a task or project leads to control over it. Not only that, but as the work advances, others need you increasingly, and so must involve you in decision making. This all creates power. A college, for example, facing a budget crisis undertook a major restructuring exercise. The staffing officer took the trouble to master the complex formulae for calculating severance benefits. He suddenly became a key figure, as only he could supply the information essential for decision making. The staffing officer was therefore invited to all the confidential meetings of the college directorate, which enabled him to influence the restructuring exercise. Furthermore, having thus earned the respect of his senior colleagues he became a permanent member of the college directorate.

Obviously it is necessary to guard against being exploited. The best advice is to direct your services towards those most likely to influence your promotion, or who you wish to be noticed by. Moreover, it is important to recognize that to undertake a task is to become responsible for it. If things turn out badly, it only sounds plaintive to point out that it was not really your job. Be careful, therefore, in what you commit yourself to. One way of assessing the value of an opportunity is to ask yourself:

what might this become?

Blue-chip openings are new ventures with long-term potential and a reasonable prospect of a successful launch, especially if they involve the acquisition of specialist skills and knowledge. The projects to avoid are those which have a history of failure, or which are held in low esteem. For example, in one of my previous organizations the employee suggestion scheme was regarded by senior managers as an embarrassment. Consequently, anyone who became identified with it was tacitly devalued by their peers and seniors.

Accepting additional responsibility

Accepting additional responsibility is a variation upon the preceding theme of doing the work. As the case of the data base manager earlier in this chapter showed, increasing your experience and broadening your power base is an excellent means of advancement.

You can create your own luck through preparation. Look around: who in the organization is likely to leave; where do problems exist; what is your boss doing that you could be doing? Having identified potential opportunities, make sure you are ready to seize them when the time comes. Learn what you can about the various possible roles, and ingratiate yourself with the existing post-holders. Let it be known that you wish to broaden your experience, though be discreet, as overt ambition stimulates hostility and resistance.

When the chance comes, offer your services immediately, or better still, assume the role. Your superiors are unlikely to remove you; to them it is one less problem to worry about. It is emphasized that this is not the time to start discussing a salary enhancement. (It is different if the other party needs you; it is assumed here that your position is tenuous.) By all means obtain a commitment if you can, but be prepared to sacrifice short-term advantage.

It should be noted that deputizing is double-edged. It can increase the possibility of being appointed to the job, or can destroy it. This is because tenure beyond the 'honeymoon' period exposes the negative as well as positive aspects of your performance. Psychology informs us that people prefer positively-framed problems to negatively-framed ones.[8] In this context a positively-framed problem is:

> *the possibility of a successful appointment with*
> *an unknown candidate.*

A negatively-framed problem is:

> *the certainty of appointing someone with known limitations.*

Power-seekers need to weigh matters very carefully in the light of this information. The longer the exposure and the more difficult the job, the greater the risk in deputizing. Why not let your rival do it?

Supporting others

The workplace can be unpleasant, even frightening. Supporting others, in the role of confessor, is a means to power because of the information which confessors became privy to. The role of confessor can be developed quickly and easily by:

- listening to everyone;
- gossiping to no one.

The second point is critical. After all, if someone divulges confidences to you, you can expect them to do the same with any secrets you entrust to them.

Seizing the initiative

Possession of the initiative can be a critical factor in determining outcomes. For that reason, power-seekers are advised to retain the initiative. Strangely enough, people are often reluctant to avail themselves of this advantage. They prefer to wait and see what the other party does. This is a mistake, because it affords the other party the opportunity to do something detrimental to your interests. So-called 'softly softly' approaches to rescuing hostages, for example, have been criticized because they leave the initiative with the terrorists, which results in captives being killed before the authorities decide to intervene.

The power of initiative comes from being first to fill the vacuum. It is surprising the difference even small things, such as suggesting a date for a meeting, or deciding not to wait for someone else to reply to a letter, can make to outcomes. At the very least it can lead to a more convenient life. Moreover, sometimes initiatives such as organizing a discussion, declaring a crisis, and so forth, can prove decisive. For example, an instruction was once issued to close down immediately some loss-making laundries. The reason for speed was to prevent the trade unions from mobilizing opposition. It was recognized, however, that given the throughput, ie the amount of wet washing on the premises, this decision could not be implemented. Instead, the management took the initiative and declared the laundries 'closed'. By 'closed' they meant that no further orders would be accepted, and that existing operations would be rapidly run down as work was completed. The trade unions interpreted the declaration literally and concluded that it was too late to oppose closure.

Having seized the initiative, it is vital to keep it. At the most basic level this may entail no more, for example, than arranging to be the one to make a telephone call. Sometimes, however, a little engineering is required. Here is a prize example:

A group of teachers were taking industrial action. They were due to meet with council officials in order to hear their proposals. At the pre-meeting between councillors, Labour and Conservative councillors disagreed over the terms to be offered. Having summoned the trade unions, however, everyone agreed that although no offer could now be made, it was imperative that a meeting of some sort be held.

The Leader of the Council said, 'Leave it to me', and trade union officials were duly invited into the room. It was Christmas-time and snowing. The Leader of the Council opened the proceedings: 'Ladies and gentlemen,' he said, 'I have asked you here to find out whether there has been any change in your position. Will you answer me, yes, or no?'

The trade union officials looked puzzled. 'Change in our position?' they said. 'Of course not.'

'Very well then,' said the Leader of the Council, 'I wish you a merry Christmas.'

'Merry Christmas?' muttered one female trade union official who had staggered into the meeting, laden with shopping bags brushing snowflakes from her coat. 'You mean he's dragged us all this way just to say "Merry Christmas!" '

The central theme of this book is that if you wait for someone to confer power upon you, you will wait forever, but, if you assume control, seldom will anyone stop you.

A group of departmental personnel officers, for example, used to meet fortnightly for a pub-lunch and a discussion of professional matters. When a new director of personnel was appointed, he asked if he could attend the meeting. (He had to ask, as departmental personnel officers did not report to him.) Within weeks of the director joining the group, some of the meetings began to be held in his office. Then, all the meetings were held there. Formal agenda and minutes were instituted, membership was expanded, and attendance became mandatory. Beer and sandwiches became a thing of the past as the director assumed control.

A vital point in taking initiative is:

> *never ask if you can do something; do it.*

It is always easier for others to say 'No' than to say 'Yes'. A training officer, for instance, took the initiative to produce a new-style employee handbook. When he showed the finished product to his manager the latter said, 'If you had asked me whether we should produce this, I would have said, "No". Now that I've seen it, I say "Why didn't we do this years ago?" '

Resist the temptation to boast of your intentions. Admiration soon sours if delivery fails. A lecturer once tried to advance his career by proclaiming he would obtain exemption from the examinations of a professional institute for one of the college courses. Having committed himself, the lecturer was subsequently horrified to discover what was involved in the task, (which had now become one of his formal objectives). Three years later it was an objective in which he had failed, and been seen to fail. Had he done his homework before raising expectations, the fiasco could have been avoided, and he could have found a more profitable outlet for his energies.

The power of deeds done

Opposition parties may criticize government decisions. Once in power, however, they seldom reverse them. This is partly because implementing a decision is rather like baking a cake. The chemical changes undergone in the oven by the eggs, flour and butter are irreversible. The passage of time alone may preclude reversion to the status quo. As the Chinese proverb reminds us, no one can bathe in the same river twice. This may serve power-seekers, in that:

> *what is done, is done.*

Once the lap-top computers have been bought, they cannot be

returned. Money, once spent, is spent. Once a contract has been awarded, whatever the objections, it is a case of 'If it's signed it's signed'. (Incidentally, if the contract is not signed, or if the order has not yet been processed, you can still pretend it is too late to stop it.) In other words, power-seekers can get what they want simply by acting. Again, power may be there simply for the taking.

Exercising such power requires a cost/benefit analysis. A balance must be struck between the potential gains and the potential consequences once the deed is discovered. Be careful if you have enemies, as you may be handing them the very opportunity they are seeking. On the other hand, bear in mind that those in authority are often well aware that the rules are silly and/or do not care anyway. If they know what you are doing they must intervene, therefore they would often rather not know. Once you know something is forbidden, you must either desist, or risk breaking the rules. If you just get on with it, the worst that may happen is that someone says, 'Tut, tut, don't do it again.' In that case, apologize humbly and carry on.

Summary

- Power can be made from nothing, ie by filling a vacuum.

- Organizations consist of three zones:
  - the permitted
  - the discretionary
  - the forbidden.

- Some discretion always exists, even in the most tightly-controlled organizations.

- Power can be created by exploiting discretion.

- Power is often created simply by assuming control.

- Assumed power is rarely challenged, but eventually legitimized.

- Luck can be created by seeking potential opportunities and preparing for them.

- Energy is a power-seeker's most valuable asset.

- Energy must be carefully directed, however, otherwise it can be counter-productive.

- Energy can be used to create power by:

    — managing the way you do your job
    — time management
    — doing the work
    — accepting extra responsibility
    — supporting others
    — seizing and retaining the initiative.

- Deputizing is risky because it exposes weaknesses.

- Never ask if you can do something, just do it.

- Resist the temptation to boast about what you intend to do.

- A *fait accompli* is unlikely to be reversed.

- Those in authority would often rather not know what you are doing.

POWER CREATION QUESTIONNAIRE

Having read the chapter, re-test yourself:

1. **A new employee looks lost and unhappy. Do you:**

    a) take him under your wing
    b) take him to the manager
    c) send him back to the personnel office
    d) ignore him?

2. **Normal practice is to appoint new staff at the bottom of the salary scale. You wish to appoint above this level. The rule-book says you have 'discretion to vary normal arrangements in exceptional circumstances'. Do you:**

    a) check with the personnel office what 'exceptional circumstances' means
    b) ask the personnel office for a ruling
    c) discuss it with the chief executive
    d) decide for yourself that the circumstances are exceptional, and offer more than the bottom of the scale?

3. **There has been a serious flood in the building over the weekend; consequently your own office is uninhabitable. There is a vacant office downstairs which you have always coveted. Do you:**

    a) move in immediately
    b) wait a day or two and then move in
    c) ask if you can use the office temporarily
    d) wait and see what the plans are?

4. **You have been asked to write a short article for a trade journal, which is a good opportunity to get your name publicized. Do you:**

    a) write down whatever comes into your head and send it off
    b) write down whatever comes into your head but then work at it
    c) jot down a few ideas and then do some research
    d) get someone else to research it?

5. **A sales representative from an employment and management consultancy firm seeks an appointment with you.**

Do you:

    a) give him half an hour
    b) ask someone else to see him
    c) ask to see a brochure first
    d) decline?

6. **A government agency has enquired about purchasing one of your products. They sound as if they are almost ready to sign a contract which could result in huge orders. Do you:**

    a) tell your boss that all his problems are solved
    b) say nothing to anyone and await developments
    c) tell your boss that some progress has been made and devote all your time to clinching the contract
    d) say nothing, and renew your efforts to secure business elsewhere?

7. **You want to buy a piece of project management software costing £800. Financial regulations state that all orders for non-emergency items must be placed centrally, which takes a long time and often results in endless questioning and argument. Do you:**

    a) get what you need and be prepared to defend your actions later
    b) sit down with a cup of coffee and the rule-book and see if there is a way round the problem
    c) try and obtain an exemption
    d) place an order in the proper way?

8. **You have a choice of how you spend a day. Assuming your objective is to increase power, which option would you select:**

    a) go through the budget making sure everything is on target
    b) use the opportunity to catch up on outstanding tasks
    c) attend a conference
    d) 'walk the floor'?

9. **A major contract is due for renewal. Do you:**

    a) routinely invite suppliers to tender
    b) arrange to meet prospective contractors informally
    c) delegate the work but ask to be kept informed
    d) delegate the whole thing and forget about it?

10. **Your manager is absent long-term sick with a stress-related illness as a direct result of the problems of managing the department. Do you:**

    a) volunteer to deputize at once
    b) stand back and let your rival volunteer
    c) decide you will deputize if asked
    d) wait to see if you are asked and then think about it?

Answers overleaf.

Answers to questionnaire

1. **a**.

2. **d** — you have discretion, use it. Why give the personnel department power?

3. **a** — no one will like you for it, but it is the surest way to get what you want.

4. **c** — create your own luck by doing that little bit more.

5. **a** — you never know, he might offer you a job.

6. **d** — no public bureaucracy moves that fast.

7. **b** — it depends how you interpret 'non-urgent'.

8. **c** — conferences are a good way of learning things and making new contacts. If you dislike conferences, walk the floor instead.

9. **b** — you have power, build on it.

10. **b**.

Score before reading chapter: ——

Score after reading chapter: ——

References

1. Lukes, S (1974) *Power: A Radical View*, Macmillan, London.
2. Brown, W (1971) *Organization*, Heinemann, London.
3. Stewart, M (1989) 'Studies of managerial jobs and behaviour: the ways forward,' *Journal of Management Studies*, 26(1), pp. 1–10.
4. Hales, C P (1986) 'What do managers do? A critical review,' *Journal of Management Studies*, 23(1), pp. 88–115.
5. McLaverty, P and Drummond, H (1991) 'The impact of effort in organizations', *Working Paper Series*, Manchester Business School.
6. Bacharach, P and Lawler, E (1980) *Power and Politics in Organizations*, Josey-Bass, San Fransisco.
7. Watzlawick, P, Weakland, J H, Fisch, R (1974) *Change: Principles of Problem Formation and Resolution*, Norton, New York.
8. Bazerman, M H (1990) *Judgement in Managerial Decision Making*, John Wiley, New York.

3

Authority is power

Before reading this chapter, answer the following questions.

1. **Some new office furniture has arrived and your staff are squabbling over who gets what. Do you:**

    a) say you will decide according to greatest need
    b) suggest they draw lots for it
    c) threaten to send the whole lot back if there is any more argument
    d) leave them to argue?

2. **One of your staff has resigned following a personality clash with another employee who also reports to you. You are aware that the latter is a trouble-maker. Do you:**

    a) take formal disciplinary action against him if he is partly to blame
    b) transfer him as a punishment
    c) make veiled threats
    d) let it drop?

3. **An employee refuses to carry out an instruction. Do you:**

    a) secretly avow revenge
    b) try and persuade him
    c) find out what the problem is but insist upon obedience
    d) get a more senior manager to enforce your authority?

4. **What colour suit would you choose to wear to an important meeting?**

    a) grey
    b) blue

c) black
d) green.

5. **What sort of pen do you normally use?**

   a) standard office issue
   b) a much-chewed pencil
   c) a cheap fountain pen or biro
   d) the best you can afford.

6. **Which of the following most closely describes your brief-case?**

   a) contains a few essential files neatly ordered, one or two pens in their slots and a few essentials such as timetables, charts etc neatly held in their slots
   b) contains everything you might need such as A4 pads, pens, pencils, files, spare money, extra credit cards, a novel, separate files containing vital facts, figures, contacts etc.
   c) a disorganized glory-hole
   d) never carry a briefcase, make do with a plastic carrier-bag.

7. **Which of the following jobs would you prefer?**

   a) one with lots of money
   b) one that you enjoy
   c) one with lots of power
   d) one with lots of money and lots of power.

8. **Which of the following would you choose to travel to work in?**

   a) an expensive Ford saloon
   b) a bicycle
   c) a Morgan sports car
   d) a Vauxhall Cavalier.

9. **You need to sound out a trade union official on a delicate matter. Would you:**

   a) include it as part of the agenda on the regular formal meeting
   b) mention it next time he pops in for a chat
   c) arrange to see him specially
   d) catch him on the corridor some time?

10. **Now that you are rising to eminence as a scientist and writer, would you describe yourself as:**

a) Peter Smith
b) Peter Smith, B.Sc., Ph.D.
c) Dr Peter Smith
d) Dr Peter Smith, B.Sc., Ph.D?

Authority is the most obvious source of power in organizations, yet often the most neglected. Authority is defined as where:

- one party has a right to command, and
- the other has an obligation to obey.[1]

Authority rests upon the idea of legitimacy — strong men will obey weaker men,[2] because society tacitly acknowledges that the rule of law is essential for the general good and enforces it accordingly.

In organizations, the concept of authority is expressed as the right to manage. The right to manage is acknowledged in law. Broadly speaking, it empowers managers to make decisions and issue instructions in accordance with operational needs. The right to manage applies from supervisory to board level. It obliges employees to:

- obey;
- observe fidelity;
- exercise reasonable skill and care in going about their work.

Obedience means that the manager or supervisor has a right to issue instructions, allocate work, control timekeeping, set standards of conduct and performance etc, and the employee is obliged to comply with these. *Fidelity* refers to the employer's right to receive faithful service, ie the employee is obliged to behave honestly, not to make a secret profit from his employment, or to compete with his employer. The obligation to exercise reasonable skill and care means just what it says. The law expects employees to give all tasks proper attention, to work diligently and conscientiously.

The role of authority

Despite management's clear right to manage, it is surprising how many managers, at all levels, hesitate to use their authority. Experience suggests this is probably because of fear of looking foolish if their authority is successfully challenged. Managers can be confident, however, that provided their instructions are operationally necessary, and conveyed in a reasonable manner, no basis for challenge exists. An employee who refuses to carry out an instruction, or who is uncooperative or obstructive, can be dismissed provided proper disciplinary procedures are observed — a point which seems to be lost upon some managers, who make matters worse by creating fear and suspicion through the use of underhand tactics.[3]

Another common reason for reluctance to enforce control is the fear of incurring hostility. In fact, the opposite is true:

> *authority is vital to organizational stability and the quality of working life.*

Few things frustrate employees more than ambiguity, such as:

- being unclear about what is permissible
- being unclear about what is expected of them
- being unable to progress because they are unable to obtain clear authorization.

Even people at the highest levels need instructions. Authority provides a framework for order and responsible management. It gives shape and meaning to the organization and protects employees. Imagine your own work place without anyone in charge: what would happen after the initial euphoria subsided? People would start to bicker over who did what; everyone would behave as they pleased, regardless of danger, discomfort or inconvenience to others. As discipline crumbled, the more powerful personalities would assume control. Orders, however unfair or unwise, would be enforced by any means the power-holders chose, for they would be accountable to no one.

Fear of informal dominance is often at the root of conflict between groups and individuals. An important function of management is to exercise authority in order to ensure the organization functions effectively. Two groups of managers, for example, both opposed a proposal to merge their respective site-based administrative support staff into one centralized group. The aim of the merger was to eliminate duplication and improve communications. The leader sensed that the reason for the resistance was the fear by both groups that the other would assume control of the administrative staff. Having succeeded in getting both groups to admit their feelings, he then emphasized that the new administrative group would report to him. Far from resenting this assertion of authority, the fears of both groups were relieved, thus enabling the proposal to be implemented.

How to create an air of authority

In theory, each manager's authority is formally limited and prescribed.
In practice:

impressions of authority can be manipulated to increase power.

Goffman reminds us that the origin of the word 'person' is the Latin
word for mask.[4] As in all power relations, perceptions of authority rest
not upon reality, but on what the other party believes. Belief can be
manipulated by impression management. Impression management in
this context means:

fulfilling the stereotype; or better still,
going beyond it.[5]

Fulfilling the stereotype begins with looking the part. This means
creating the right impression through manipulating appearances such
as:

- clothes
- cars
- office decor and furnishings.

Dress

When His Royal Highness the Prince of Wales visited my home town a
few years ago, the local press subsequently reported that the children
from an infant school who had turned out to see him were disappointed that the Prince had not worn his crown. (One small fellow is
reported to have been reduced to tears, so acute was his unfulfilment.)

As this tale shows, dress is a vitally important aspect of conforming
to the stereotype. Maybe appearances should not matter; the point is,
no matter how good you are at your job, unless you look the part, others
will find it hard to believe in you. Imagine two solicitors, for instance:
one wearing a pair of jeans and the other a pin-stripe suit. Which one
are you most likely to trust?

Strict codes of dress are fairly rare in management, and so it can be
difficult to know what is appropriate. One way of solving the problem
is to emulate the styles and standards of the successful people around
you, and better still to improve upon them. (See chapter eight, though,
for advice on when it is wise to underdress.) Furthermore:

1. More expensive clothes are generally more imposing than cheaper
   ones, so buy the best you can afford.

2. Choose styles which make you feel smart.

3. Dark blue is the most powerful colour.[6]

4. Ensure that accessories are of the same standard.

Distance helps maintain authority, and clothes can function as distancing mechanisms. Uniforms, wigs, gowns, robes and so forth are worn for this purpose. Business suits can create a similar effect. The main thing to ensure is that you feel smart in what you wear, so as to maximize your self-confidence. Research evidence shows that smart dress boosts self-esteem, and vice versa.[7] This probably explains the reluctance of British managers to emulate their Japanese counterparts by wearing uniforms.

It is not just what you wear that creates an impact, but how you wear it. At the risk of stating the obvious, expensive clothes are wasted if they looked as if they have been tossed on with a pitchfork, or are creased or stained.

Although people are deceived by appearances, they do search for inconsistencies and subtle signs which give the other party away, such as odd socks or a frayed collar.[8] Countless fraudulent social climbers have been undone by lapses such as a momentary slip of accent, lighting a cigar the wrong way, mispronunciation of a word. Tailors once gauged customers by how they asked for a top hat. Pretenders invariably asked for a 'top hat'. Only a genuine aristocrat would ask for a 'topper'.

This explains why accessories are important. By 'accessories' is meant not just shoes and gloves, but all props, including briefcases, pens, personal organizers, perfume and so on. Accessories should match the style and quality of your outfit. A top quality pin-stripe suit calls for a calf leather-bound document case and Montblanc fountain pen. Although this sounds like snobbery and conspicuous materialism, the thing to remember is that people notice these things and are impressed by them.

If the reader's income, like the author's, does not support such lavishness, buy the best you can afford and be especially conscious of how you use it. For example, a bulging personal organizer cuts a poor impression compared with one neatly kept. Similarly a briefcase crammed full of rubbish and crisp-packets is hardly suggestive of someone in control.

That said, do not worry too much about people seeing through the image. It is impossible to fool everyone. Those close to you are bound to observe your weaknesses. For the few that know you, there are many more who do not, and are impressed.

Cars

Cars too convey impressions. In these days of mass utility and company cars, positive distinction is hard to achieve. If you are able to invest in an unusual and exciting vehicle, then do. At the very least, guard against creating a negative impression. A senior manager who drove an old dilapidated van shared the same image as the vehicle: underpowered, unenthusiastic, and overdue for the scrap heap. Personalized registration plates are an increasingly popular means of emphasizing individuality. It is a matter of taste, of course, but experience suggests that they tend to attract more ridicule than admiration on all but the rarest or most expensive motors, especially the cheaper plates.

Office furniture and layout

Office furniture and lay-out are assets which can be used to create power. Decor can be used to create an impression as follows:

1. Blue — dominance and status.
2. White — space and freedom.
3. Red — fear, through connotations of blood.[9]

A large office always conveys an impression of power, provided it is not so large that the occupant looks lost or small in it. Power takes time to develop; to acquire too much too soon in the way of trappings can be counter-productive if the power-seeker has yet to develop the personal stature to match his surroundings. It is like a learner driver practising with a turbocharged car.

In any case, much can be done with a small office or even a desk in an open-plan office and minimal resources. Creating a personalized atmosphere through the use of plants, photographs, pictures and so on creates power through emphasizing individuality, and displaying a determination to put your stamp on the organization. A piece of coal, epaulettes, an engine component, a wooden shuttle or other makeshift paper weight can be used to symbolize achievement and determination to achieve. Imagine, for instance, receiving a sales representative. He asks you a bit about yourself. Contrast the conventional, 'Oh started off in purchasing then moved round about, worked abroad for a couple of years', with, 'You see that frame: well the sheet in there is the first order I won as junior sales rep'.

Symbols such as these not only create power, they perpetuate it as they evolve into a kind of personal legend. In the case of the sales representative referred to in the previous paragraph, imagine the following press release:

> The first thing you notice when you walk into his office is a framed copy of the first order he took as a junior salesman. The BMW parked outside suggests he has come a long way since he first pedalled round the town on a bicycle looking for customers. 'I keep it to remind me that you can sell against the competition,' he explains. 'Whenever someone tells me things are getting too tough I point to it and say, "Get on your bike." '

Legends do not by themselves guarantee wealth, power and success, but they are often the precursor to achievement. The following exercise may help you identify one:

Exercise: Create your own legend

1. List as many achievements as you can remember. They may be big or small, such as winning a match, passing a driving test, buying a bargain, and so on.

2. List as many important things that have happened to you as you can remember, pleasant or unpleasant.

3. Examine both lists, and highlight the achievements and/or events which have significantly influenced your career.

4. Select one which (a), appeals to you, and (b), can be symbolized in some way.

5. Install the symbol, and start drawing attention to it.

It does not matter if what you identify is only tangentially related to this exercise. All tales crystallize and grow with the telling. The value of searching one's memory is that people are often surprised by what they have achieved, even in the very early stages of their career, and by the curious and sometimes negative hinges upon which fate turns. Failing an examination, for example, though a disaster at the time, may subsequently prove a blessing in disguise because it forces the individual into a career in which he becomes extremely successful. (See the final chapter for a further discussion about negative influences.)

Returning to the topic of office furnishings, a desk facing entrants is always powerful, as it commands the room, which explains why it is the most common choice of position. A desk tucked in a corner, facing the wall, implies you do not need the security of a load of wood in front of you. It is disconcerting to others, because it is unconventional and therefore leaves them uncertain as to how to take you, and so gives you an edge.

Meetings-tables can be manipulated to increase or decrease distance. To dominate or intimidate, sit at the top. If you want people to relax and lower their guard, however, sit casually in the middle, as informality reduces tension.

A suite of easy chairs facilitates intimacy. I knew of a trade union official who made a point of avoiding them, presumably for fear of being too closely identified with the management. Eventually, however, he succumbed. To this day, I have never discovered whether this signified the development of trust, or just that he discovered how much more comfortable they were! They *were* comfortable too, so much so that a colleague became wont to call in for a chat — very useful.

Additionally, the office environment must look the part. Returning to the example of the solicitor: which is more reassuring, a bright modern air-conditioned office replete with tubular furniture and a personal computer, or an old-fashioned desk, chair and lamp, bundles of papers tied with pink tape and rows and rows of deed boxes marked 'Blenkinsop Deceased'?

Distinction increases authority

Looking the part will take you a long way; doing so with distinction is even better. The popular disc jockey Jimmy Saville made an impression early in his career by dying his hair both black and white, zebra crossing style. The pop singer Sandy Shaw likewise made a point of appearing without shoes. Robin Day the television presenter is known for his spotted bow tie.

The device must be consistent with your occupation. Robin Day, for instance, would not have been taken seriously had he dyed his hair like Jimmy Saville's. Likewise, Jimmy Saville would not have improved his prospects by appearing in a formal suit. There is a fine line between distinction and deviancy.

One way of creating distinction is to make yourself known for a particular attribute, be it charm, intelligence, forcefulness, or whatever. People tend to label others: find out what your label is, and if you like it, emphasize it. For example:

- 'works hard'
- 'cares about his staff'

- 'cares about the job'
- 'is very intelligent'
- 'not afraid to make a decision'
- 'knows what he is doing'
- 'very committed'
- 'always fair'
- 'always listens'.

The problem with virtue is that it is boring. Again, without shading into deviancy, make yourself interesting by cultivating a modicum of vice, such as:

- 'always late for meetings'
- 'always bad-tempered first thing'
- 'the unions didn't like him'
- 'could be moody'
- 'not one to suffer fools'
- 'he was a bit of a rogue'
- 'if he wanted something, that was it'.

No one is perfect, and you might as well control the negative as well as the positive perceptions others have of you. By so doing, you arrive at a balance such as:

- 'he could be moody, but he was always fair'
- 'he was a bit of a rogue, but he cared'
- 'he knew what he was doing, that's why the unions didn't like him'.

A sense of humour should be kept well under control. The famous and successful are almost invariably solemn, and often pompous and sanctimonious. This explains why fledgling lawyers, accountants and stockbrokers typically try and make themselves look and sound ten years older. Although weighty gestures and mannerisms such as the furrowed brow, staring at the floor and so on often appear comical when practised by young people, they become extremely powerful in time.[10]

For the exceptional only

One way of making yourself distinct is to shun a conventional approach completely. In a room full of blue pin-striped officials, the individual in the rust-coloured jacket and jeans stands out. Omitting designatory letters where designatory letters are the norm captures attention. Such a strategy will only work if your whole performance is exceptional, and even then it is risky because it defies the stereotype and borders on deviance. However, if it works, it works very well indeed, because it reinforces the image that you really are outstanding.

Summary

- Authority is an important source of power in organizations.

- Authority is defined as a right to command matched by an obligation to obey.

- All managers, from supervisory to board level have a right to manage.

- Without authority, organizations would lapse into anarchy.

- In theory, every manager's authority is fixed. In reality, it can be enhanced by impression management.

- Impression management begins by looking the part.

- Clothes and high-status furnishings can be used as distancing mechanisms.

- Even a desk in an open-plan office can be used to create power.

- Create and symbolize a legend about yourself.

- Office furnishings can be arranged and used to facilitate dominance, or reduce tension. They too should look the part.

AUTHORITY QUESTIONNAIRE

Having read the chapter, re-test yourself:

1. **Some new office furniture has arrived and your staff are squabbling over who gets what. Do you:**

    a) say you will decide according to greatest need
    b) suggest they draw lots for it
    c) threaten to send the whole lot back if there is any more argument
    d) leave them to argue?

2. **One of your staff has resigned following a personality clash with another employee who also reports to you. You are aware that the latter is a trouble-maker. Do you:**

    a) take formal disciplinary action against him if he is partly to blame
    b) transfer him as a punishment
    c) make veiled threats
    d) let it drop?

3. **An employee refuses to carry out an instruction. Do you:**

    a) secretly avow revenge
    b) try and persuade him
    c) find out what the problem is but insist upon obedience
    d) get a more senior manager to enforce your authority?

4. **What colour suit would you choose to wear for an important meeting?**

    a) grey
    b) blue
    c) black
    d) green.

5. **What sort of pen do you normally use?**

    a) standard office issue
    b) a much-chewed pencil
    c) a cheap fountain pen or biro
    d) the best you can afford.

6. **Which of the following most closely describes your brief-case?**

    a) contains a few essential files neatly ordered, one or two pens in their slots and a few essentials such as timetables, charts etc neatly held in their slots
    b) contains everything you might need such as A4 pads, pens, pencils, files, spare money, extra credit cards, a novel, separate files containing vital facts, figures, contacts etc.
    c) a disorganized glory-hole
    d) never carry a briefcase, make do with a plastic carrier-bag.

7. **Which of the following jobs would you prefer?**

    a) one with lots of money
    b) one that you enjoy
    c) one with lots of power
    d) one with lots of money and lots of power.

8. **Which of the following would you choose to travel to work in?**

    a) an expensive Ford saloon
    b) a bicycle
    c) a Morgan sports car
    d) a Vauxhall Cavalier.

9. **You need to sound out a trade union official on a delicate matter. Would you:**

    a) include it as part of the agenda on the regular formal meeting
    b) mention it next time he pops in for a chat
    c) arrange to see him specially
    d) catch him on the corridor some time?

10. **Now that you are rising to eminence as a scientist and writer, would you describe yourself as:**

    a) Peter Smith
    b) Peter Smith, B.Sc., Ph.D.
    c) Dr Peter Smith
    d) Dr Peter Smith, B.Sc., Ph.D?

Answers overleaf.

Answers to questionnaire

1. **a** — someone has to say who gets what in the end.

2. **a** — it sounds drastic, but the employee must understand that his behaviour has caused concern. Underhand methods only make the problem worse.

3. **c** — you can and should insist upon full performance.

4. **b**.

5. **d** is the best choice.

6. **a** the most impressive. B is the style of people who think they are great organizers but actually clutter their lives with too much detail. C has a kind of honest charm, but remember to keep the case closed. D is the type most likely to be jealous of others' success.

7. **b** is the only option for real and sustained success. Without it you could be on your way to a nervous breakdown — seriously.

8. **c**.

9. **b** — you need to be sure he is relaxed, attentive and that there is time for discussion.

10. **a** — eminent people do not need props. If that feels uncomfortable then B or C. D is belt and braces.

Score before reading chapter: ——

Score after reading chapter: ——

References

1. Wrong, D H (1979) *Power, Its Forms, Bases and Uses*, Basil Blackwell, Oxford.
2. Weber, M (1947) *Economy and Society*, Bedminster, New York.
3. See Drummond, H (1990) *Managing Difficult Staff: Effective Procedures and the Law*, Kogan Page, London, for a detailed explanation of managerial powers, and advice on how to exercise these.
4. Goffman, E (1959) *The Presentation of Self in Everyday Life*, Doubleday Anchor, New York.
5. Schlenker, B R (1980) *Impression Management*, Brooks Cole, California.

6. Korda, M (1976) *Power*, Ballantine Books, New York.
7. Schlenker, op. cit.
8. Goffman, op. cit.
9. Korda, op. cit.
10. Korda, op. cit.

4

Acting the part

Can you act the part? Test your skill by answering the following questions:

1. **Which most closely describes you?**

    a) even-tempered
    b) easygoing
    c) a little bit moody
    d) never the same two days together.

2. **When the telephone rings do you:**

    a) always answer immediately
    b) always let it ring at least five times
    c) answer only if you know who the caller is
    d) drown the apparatus in a bucket of water?

3. **How do you answer the telephone?**

    a) 'Hello'
    b) give the number
    c) say your name
    d) b or c and add 'Good morning/good afternoon'.

4. **When callers arrive, do you normally:**

    a) show them in immediately
    b) get your secretary to show them in immediately
    c) keep them waiting a few minutes
    d) disappear out of the other door?

5. **You wish to convey your displeasure to a colleague forcefully. Do you:**

a) go and see him in his office
b) ask him to come and see you
c) catch him in the car park
d) write an angry memo?

6. **You meet someone attractive at a conference. Do you:**

   a) stay on an extra day
   b) leave when you are due to leave
   c) leave after the other person leaves
   d) leave a day before you want to?

7. **A trade union convener wants you to extend an employee's sick-pay. You feel he has a strong case. Do you say:**

   a) 'OK, no problem'
   b) 'I suppose so'
   c) 'I will pay it if you can convince me that there is a case'
   d) 'Very well, but I hope you realize how much this is costing'?

8. **Someone telephones to enquire about a refund claim. Would you say:**

   a) 'I will sign it'
   b) 'I will make sure it's processed'
   c) 'It's being dealt with'
   d) 'What refund?'

9. **A prestigious project which you are associated with is showing signs of crumbling. Do you:**

   a) quietly disown the venture
   b) move swiftly to the rescue
   c) wait and see what happens before making a fuss
   d) quietly analyze the position before making a decision on whether to continue?

10. **You are worried that you might begin to stammer when making a speech to an important audience. Do you:**

    a) develop a diplomatic illness
    b) tell the audience you are nervous
    c) overcome the problem by conscious effort of will
    d) during rehearsals, make yourself stammer as much as possible?

Bertolt Brecht said, 'It is not the play but the performance that is the real purpose of all one's efforts'.[1] It is not enough just to look the part, you have to act it as well. Acting the part not only assures credibility; good acting is a way of acquiring power. Act powerful and you become powerful. It is as simple as that. This chapter sets out the script.

Accessibility

Distance lends enchantment, and enchantment creates power. The monarch does not give interviews, in order to preserve the crown's mystique. Managers, too, must retain an air of mystery about themselves. Mystery:

- creates interest
- protects against manipulation
- preserves respect
- creates an edge of fear

Predictable people are susceptible to manipulation. Others learn which tunes their victims will dance to and play them accordingly. Familiarity breeds contempt. Even the most conscientious employee sooner or later takes advantage of his position. It is much easier to say 'You will' from a distance. Unpredictability creates an edge of fear, fear of the unknown. Since people can never be sure how you will react, they are more likely to treat you with respect and less likely to try and exploit you. It is a mistake to rely solely upon goodwill for, as Machiavelli observed, such is the fickle nature of man that goodwill can turn to bitter enmity overnight. Fear is the soundest basis for obtaining compliance.

The degree of distance is a matter of judgement. The aim should be to maintain reserve without becoming isolated, and to create a reputation of a volatile temperament, without it becoming a liability. Here are some suggestions for preserving mystique:

1. Restrict availability.

2. Conduct important discussions on your own territory.

3. Restrict socialization.

4. Cultivate unpredictability.

When oysters were cheap and plentiful, they were despised as food of the poor. Managers who make themselves scarce are more valued and respected than their more obliging counterparts. Teach people respect for you before they even meet you by giving the impression that you are a busy and important person. The reality is immaterial — only the performance counts. For example, a colleague once interrupted my conversation with him, saying in tones of awe, 'I have to ring Professor So And So. I've been waiting three weeks to speak to him and his secretary tells me he has a ten-minute slot in his diary.'

Note, however, that inaccessibility may result in lost opportunities. This explains why successful businessmen and women are often extremely approachable. They enjoy surprise and excitement, knowing that the humblest of callers may be the harbinger of luck:

Light the lamp, open the door wide
So the pilgrim can come in,
Gentile or Jew:
Under the rags perhaps the prophet is concealed.
(From 'Passover', in Levi, P (1888) *Collected Poems*,
tr R Feldman and B Swann, Faber & Faber, London.)

One strategy for gaining the best of both worlds is to make yourself approachable, while simultaneously controlling access through delegation and manipulation of time. You might, for example, agree to speak to a chance caller, and then pass him over to your secretary to arrange an appointment. Your secretary can then emphasize how busy you are. Even the way you answer the telephone says something about you. Let it ring at least five times, otherwise you give the impression that you are eager to receive a call.

Going into other people's offices (your own staff's especially) is an unobtrusive way of maintaining vigilance. Important discussions, however, are best held upon your own territory, where you have the psychological advantage of control. Here is how to exploit it:

1. Keep the other party waiting outside the office.

No matter how important or senior the other party is, teach them respect for you by keeping them waiting — especially if it is your first encounter. If necessary, sit idle for a few minutes. If the occasion warrants it, you can add to your air of importance by arranging for one or two staff to go in and out with worried-looking expressions.

2. Arrange to be interrupted during the discussion.

This signals to the other party that you do not regard him as important. Be careful, though, as too many interruptions will make you appear disorganized. One telephone call will suffice. Alternatively, if your aim is to flatter, you can ostentatiously give orders not to be disturbed.

You can add to the atmosphere by getting your secretary to enter the room, and, looking suitably apologetic, to say, 'Sorry but it's the chief exec/Foreign Office/*Financial Times*'; choose what you will, provided both you and the secretary can keep a straight face. On receiving this message you can look suitably bored and say to the other person, 'Would you excuse me please', meaning 'Get out.' They may not like it, but they will be impressed. (If you are forced to go into someone else's territory, you can score an advantage by arranging to receive an important telephone call there, even if it is only a ruse. You can also use it as an excuse to terminate the meeting.)

Secretaries, in my experience, enjoy the game enormously, because it makes them feel powerful too. Many are better actors than the people they work for. Do encourage them to exploit this capability.

3. Include supporters.

You can create the advantage of surprise by including supporters where the other party was expecting a cosy *tête-à-tête*, and, vice versa.

4. Take the initiative.

You have the initiative; use it. Establish command from the start by using phrases like, 'I needed to see you because . . .' or, 'I have three things to discuss with you.' You can also control the time of the meeting by indicating when it must finish. It is polite to address someone by their name, but subtly demeaning to pretend you have forgotten it. It is efficient to have all the papers to hand. Alternatively you can lower the other person's esteem by using the absence of any papers as a sign that, to you, the issue is so trivial it is not worth the effort of preparation or recording. Likewise, pretending to have forgotten about the meeting is a way of signalling how unimportant you regard the other party.

5. Facilities

You can impress the other party with your power by displaying your ability to call up files, organize coffee, obtain photocopies, and so on. Never, however, ask for a file unless you know it is there. Remember, you are acting a set-piece. The only exception to this rule is where it is expedient that the file should be elsewhere, or lost.

Exceptions to the territory rule

The two exceptions to the territory rule are:

1. Where you want the other party to feel relaxed, or,

2.   Where a dramatic gesture is appropriate.

People tend to be more relaxed in their own territory, and therefore more expansive and accommodating. When dealing with a volatile situation or seeking information or favours, it is usually best to go to the other person.

Where something unpleasant must be said, one approach is to walk into the other person's office, attack, then leave before they can reply. This not only conveys displeasure effectively: it creates a psychological edge by showing the other person that you can invade their territory at will.

Socialization should be carefully managed, especially where subordinates are concerned. Your mystique will be destroyed irreparably if you become drunk, reveal secrets, or otherwise behave inappropriately at an event. The best approach is to use socialization to emphasize distance. Contribute generously to funds, but restrict the number of invitations accepted, and always leave early. The best time to leave any event if you wish to make an impression is:

before you want to.

Pay attention to how you eat. Generally speaking, powerful people never seem to need food. Being seen eating out of a paper bag while walking round town at lunch time creates an impression *ordinare*; the chief executive seen emerging from the lift stuffing a greasy pie into his mouth can hardly complain if he is mistaken for a clerk.

Unpredictability means giving the impression of being volatile and temperamental, while actually controlling your every reaction. The possibilities are wide. For example, when someone reports failure, sometimes you react equably, other times with simulated shock or anger. You might cultivate a certain moodiness. You might enthuse about someone or some project one day, and be cool the next, or even pretend you have forgotten all about the person or the idea.

Be a king

The nature of authority can be summed up as:

use it or lose it.

Margaret Thatcher's famous declamation, 'U-turn if you want to, the lady's not for turning', epitomizes the idealized image of the leader in Western culture as someone decisive and resolute. Nothing damages politicians and managers more than to be perceived as vacillating or indecisive.[2] One of the key elements in acting out the role of leader therefore is:

to create a reputation for decisiveness.

Decisiveness makes a manager look like a leader, whatever the reality.[3] The problem is that swift decision making can be disastrous if it means that issues are not thought through properly. Self-preservation therefore demands the cultivation of an image which satisfies others, and serves as a smoke screen behind which proper analysis evaluation can take place.

An air of decisiveness can be created by:

- displaying energy;
- use of language;
- over-acting on small issues.

Each of these is now discussed in turn.

The power of energy

Energy is attractive; history says that people flocked to see King Henry II of England, such was the energy that shone in his face. His son, Richard I, known as Lionheart, owes his heroic image to his energetic leadership of the Crusades.[4] As with kings, so with managers. If you want to look successful, look energetic. Brisk speech, a brisk purposeful stride, short hair, short styled clothes all give an impression of verve. Guard against appearing childishly enthusiastic or agitated, as these behaviours are counter-productive. Aim to cultivate a certain moody impatience.

Use of language

Others will perceive you as decisive if you use decisive-sounding language.[5] Moreover, conveying an impression of control deflects potential criticism. Winston Churchill was a master of the art. Here are excerpts from one of his war speeches:

> I must, however, try to bring home to the House the extraordinary difficulties of our strategic position arising from Hitler's mastery of the European coast. These difficulties far exceed anything that was experienced in the last war. In fact, . . . at the beginning of 1940 . . . most of the high naval and air experts would have said

that the problem of supplying Britain would have become insoluble and hopeless.

> (Eade, C (1951) *Winston Spencer Churchill: War Speeches 1939-1945, Vol. 2, Cassel, London, p.2)*

Not only is Churchill's language used to reassure, but it pre-empts censure by creating the impression that national difficulties are entirely due to forces outside the government's control:

> Bound together as we are by a common purpose, the men who have joined hands in this affair put up with a lot, and I hope they will put up with a lot more. It is the duty of the Prime Minister to use the power which Parliament and the Nation have given him to drive others, and in war like this that power has to be used irrespective of anyone's feelings. If we win, nobody will care. If we lose, there will be nobody to care.

> (Eade, op. cit., p. 8)

This speech is virtually an assumption of *carte blanche*. The references 'put up with a lot' divert attention from analysis of the mistakes while the reference to power implies that the Prime Minister can and should override other counsels.

As for results, this example stands for many:

> There might be ups and downs, there might be disappointments, there would certainly be the ebb and flow of battle, ... Mistakes are made. Sometimes right things turn out wrong, and quite often wrong things turn out right.

> (Eade, op. cit., pp. 134–5)

Here language is used to pre-empt criticism, by structuring the audience's expectations. Not only are they invited to believe that disasters are inevitable, but that they are attributable to the fortunes of war. Nowhere does Churchill mention his own fallibility.

Lest readers feel that their opportunities to practise eloquence are limited, this address requires only minor amendments to make it suitable for a management situation:

> There might be ups and downs, there might be disappointments, there would certain by the ebb and flow of competition and economic climate, ... Mistakes are made. Sometimes right things turn out wrong, and quite often wrong things turn out right.

Churchill also knew the value of language in explaining away mistakes. His words on the sinking of the battleships *Prince of Wales* and *Repulse* were:

Admiral Philips was undertaking a thoroughly sound, well-considered offensive operation, not indeed free from risk, but not different in principle from many similar operations we have repeatedly carried out . . . . There is reason to believe that the loss of life has been less heavy than was at first feared.

(Eade, op. cit., p. 141)

Who says it was a sound operation? We believe it only because we are told it was. This speech too is readily convertible for use by management:

We were undertaking a thoroughly sound, well-considered project, not indeed free from risk, but not different in principle from many similar operations we have repeatedly carried out . . . . There is reason to believe that the losses are less heavy than was at first feared.

The format can be utilized to explain virtually any failure:

1. Emphasize that the plan was soundly conceived and based on precedent.

2. Point out the element of risk.

3. Reduce the tension by concluding with more optimistic figures than those first released.

Day-to-day issues too provide an excellent opportunity to exploit the power of language. For instance:

1. 'You require a *decision* on . . .'

2. 'I must give a *ruling* upon . . .'

3. 'Clearly then the *decision* rests between . . .'

4. 'The *options* are . . .'

5. 'The risks I must *choose* between are . . .'

Expressions like these can be used to make others feel that serious issues are being decided. Everyone likes to feel part of momentous events, and it is good management to engender excitement by hyping things up a little. Besides, making others feel powerful enhances your own stature.

Over-acting on small issues

Doctors say that if they save a life the patient subsequently complains that the bill is too high and the stitches hurt. To do something in five minutes for a bad headache, however, is to earn a friend for life. The same is true in management. Employees are generally more concerned about issues directly affecting them, such as canteen provision, the issue of protective clothing, and holiday rotas, than grand strategy. Clear and prompt decisions over small things are appreciated, and are another way of creating an image of decisiveness.

Emphasizing your authority

A militant trade union convener once had permission to borrow a company van to attend a meeting. While he was in the meeting, the parked vehicle was impounded by the police because it was causing an obstruction. The trade union official was horrified, because he knew the van would be needed the next day. Only the building services manager could authorize payment of monies for the van's release.

The manager could have signed a petty cash voucher immediately. Instead, he took the opportunity to emphasize his authority by pretending, through his secretary, that he was in an important meeting and could not be disturbed. The convener had no option but to wait outside his office, white-faced and wretched. Two hours later, the 'meeting' ended. Instead of signing the voucher, however, the manager then interrogated the convener at length before finally authorizing payment.

This exercise of power resulted in a subtle but permanent change in the convener's demeanour. He was never quite so militant again — at least not towards that manager. The moral of this story is:

> *when they need you, they need you.*

Ten ways to sound powerful

Any issue where authority exists to say 'yes' or 'no' is an opportunity to increase power, and one which is often wasted. Affable expressions like, 'Gimme it, I'll sign it', and, 'I'll see what I can do', are like shovelling bank-notes on to the fire. How much more powerful to say:

1. 'I will authorize payment.'

2. 'I have authority to vary the scheme in exceptional cases.'

3. 'I will pay the claim.'

4. 'I will sign it.'

5. 'If you can convince me that there is a case . . . .'

6. 'I have discretion to agree variations to the contract.'

7. 'I would need clear evidence that existing resources are being utilized to capacity.'

8. 'It is critical to me that the proposal is properly thought through.'

9. 'I have power to veto . . . .'

10. 'My strategy is to secure a market base within two years.'

'I' is the most important word. Use it wherever possible, because it implies that you, and you alone, can solve the problem. The word 'will' is powerful because it means just what it says, 'I will.' For that reason avoid the short-cut 'I'll'. The words 'power' and 'authorize' always add weight; use them liberally. Expressions like, 'If you can convince me', and 'I would need clear evidence' work because they emphasize that you sit in judgement. The word 'critical' always has a dramatic impact, while words like 'strategy' impress, partly because they are resonant of a Harvard MBA, but more particularly because they show others that you know what you are doing, and why.

How to be decisive and obstructive

A good way of thwarting others, without necessarily appearing to do so, is to discover that you are unable to do what they want. Such ostensible impotence can soon be used to create an impression of power, by the use of language such as:

1. 'I have no authority to . . . .'

2. 'It would be irresponsible of me to . . . .'

3. 'It would not be appropriate for me to . . . .'

These three phrases convey respectively impressions of authority, responsibility, and propriety. Furthermore, they are extremely difficult to challenge.

Rules are best invoked in sorrow rather than in anger. Making others feel your power by appearing deliberately obstructive creates resentment. Cry a few crocodile tears to soften the blow, and ensure that if a determined individual succeeds in overcoming the obstruction, you can say, 'Well done, I wish I'd thought of that.'

Here is a potential repertoire of crocodile tears:

1. 'Personally, I am sympathetic, but, you know the rules.'

2. 'I only wish I could.'

3. 'The problem is, I have no discretion.'

4. 'You will appreciate, I am sure, that if we do it for one, we have to do it for all.'

5. 'I've racked my brains to find a way round this, but this time I think I am stumped.'

6. 'As you know, the rules on this are applied very strictly.'

7. 'If I did that, I would be looking for another job tomorrow.'

8. 'Unfortunately there is no provision for . . . .'

9. 'I agree it seems unfair, but there is nothing I can do about it.'

10. 'It's a shame we can't do it.'

The beauty of the language tactic is that anyone can use it. Even the most junior employee can impress his power upon others by saying 'I will sign it'. It is immaterial that the matter is a routine one. Power is created by reminding the other party of their dependence. Remember:

once you start to act the part, the part eventually becomes part of you.

Just as people who feign insanity often become insane, people who cultivate an air of command eventually become powerful personalities. Like many skills it takes time to acquire. The best way of learning is to make small, easy changes, and experience the effect. The telephone is a good place to start, because you cannot see the other person and you are therefore less likely to falter.

Fielding questions

Asking questions is an excellent offensive tactic as it forces the other person on to your ground. It is equally important to be able to cope with questioning confidently. Being knowledgeable and prepared helps, but power-seekers must also be able to cope with the unexpected. Listed below are the tactics commonly used by politicians.[6]

1. Ignore the question.

2. Acknowledge the question, without answering it.

3. Question the question.

4. Attack the interviewer.

5. Decline to answer.

6. Make a political point, eg use it as an opportunity to press a claim for resources.

7. Give an incomplete answer.

8. Repeat the previous answer.

9. Claim to have already answered the question.

Taking up a new job

A new job is an excellent opportunity to change your behaviour. It is always easier to exert authority with strangers than with people who know you. When you come into a new job, you hold all the psychological advantages of fear and mystery — so use them. There is much to be said for the old dictum of beginning with a strict approach and manner. It is much easier to relax your grip later than it is to tighten it. Restrain yourself from being overly friendly at first. First impressions are the most lasting. Let yours be of a cold eye and a dark critical look.

Overcoming weaknesses

Most people have something they dislike about themselves, such as their size, weight, squinting eyes, nervous stammer, and so forth. The intuitive approach to such problems is to either conceal or overcome them. The difficulty, however, is that the solution is often worse than the problem. Loose clothes, for instance will reduce the impression of weight, but at the expense of looking untidy. Likewise, sheer effort of will may control a stammer temporarily, but if it breaks down, as it often does, the person typically stammers worse than they did before.

An approach which is counter-intuitive but is potentially extremely effective is that of deliberately emphasizing the problem. Since the real problem is fear of the problem, by deliberately stammering, shaking, and so forth, you show yourself that you can control it, and therefore that there is no longer anything to be afraid of.[7]

A variation of this theme is to turn the problem to advantage. Obesity can be used to suggest strength and dependability. Nervousness can be dressed up as super-intelligence. Forgetfulness can translate into the image of someone impatient with petty detail. Plodders can present themselves as thorough and gifted analysts.

Captain of the ship but not owner

Beware if your deputy stops sitting next to you at meetings. It may well indicate that your star is in decline. Powerful people understand the importance of dissociating themselves from lost causes. They know 'how to look away at the right moment'.[8] Looking away may mean distancing yourself by not attending meetings, not being seen with the losing party or individuals, and disclaiming involvement. The favourite expression of one of my least-endearing former bosses was:

'Of course, I haven't been closely involved.'

Staff used to joke, 'If anything goes wrong, you'll find that Mr ____ was not involved. Even if he told you to do it, he will not have been involved.' Interestingly, even though his staff knew different, outsiders invariably believed him, which underscores the point about impression management made earlier.

Penetrating the icon

Just as you act the part, so do others. One way of 'penetrating the icon' is to look not at the image before you, but to imagine the person as he or she was as a little boy. The soft-spoken, accomplished Oxbridge graduate might have been the victim of playground bullies. If so, he probably fears confrontations. You can calculate that the grown man probably survives in the same way that he did as a schoolboy, ie by acting as a sneak and/or seeking the protection of older boys. Likewise, imagine the rugged handsome man as he was in shorts and National Health Billy Bunter glasses. Nine-tenths of the noise he makes is a cover for his feelings of inferiority. What he needs is someone to cuddle him and tell him everything is going to all right. The best way to find out what others were like as children is to ask them. They will probably enjoy telling you. Anyone who went to school with them is also worth talking to.

Summary

- In addition to looking the part, you must also act it.

- Always retain a slight air of mystery about yourself.

- Scarcity creates value; never make yourself too readily available.

- Conduct important discussions on your territory, unless you want the other party to be especially relaxed or want to invade his.

- Teach callers respect by making them wait for you, staging interruptions, demonstrating your efficiency and seizing the initiative.

- Restrict socialization, especially where subordinates are concerned.

- Stop people from taking advantage by making yourself unpredictable.

- Decisiveness makes a manager look like a leader.

- Energy, language and over-acting can be used to create an air of mastery.

- When others need you, make them wait.

- Expressions like, 'I will sign . . . , and 'I will authorize . . .' remind others that you are in control.

- Once you start to act the part, it becomes part of you.

- A new job is an excellent opportunity to launch a new image.

- Act austerely when meeting new staff. You can always relax later.

- One way of overcoming a problem is to deliberately exaggerate it.

- Never become identified with losing causes.

- When others try and impress you with their power, visualize them as children.

ACTING THE PART QUESTIONNAIRE

Having read the chapter, test yourself again:

1. Which most closely describes you?

   a) even-tempered
   b) easygoing
   c) a little bit moody
   d) never the same two days together.

2. When the telephone rings do you:

   a) always answer immediately
   b) always let it ring at least five times
   c) answer only if you know who the caller is
   d) drown the apparatus in a bucket of water?

3. How do you answer the telephone?

   a) 'Hello'
   b) give the number
   c) say your name
   d) b or c and add 'Good morning/good afternoon.'

4. When callers arrive do you normally:

   a) show them in immediately
   b) get your secretary to show them in immediately
   c) keep them waiting a few minutes
   d) disappear out of the other door?

5. You wish to convey your displeasure to a colleague forcefully. Do you:

   a) go and see him in his office
   b) ask him to come and see you
   c) catch him in the car park
   d) write an angry memo?

6. You meet someone attractive at a conference. Do you:

   a) stay on an extra day
   b) leave when you are due to leave
   c) leave after the other person leaves
   d) leave a day before you want to?

7. **A trade union convener wants you to extend an employee's sick pay. You feel he has a strong case. Do you say:**

   a) 'OK, no problem'
   b) 'I suppose so'
   c) 'I will pay it if you can convince me that there is a case.'
   d) 'Very well, but I hope you realize how much this is costing.'

8. **Someone telephones to enquire about a refund claim. Would you say:**

   a) 'I will sign it'
   b) 'I will make sure it's processed.'
   c) 'It's being dealt with'
   d) 'What refund?'

9. **A prestigious project which you are associated with is showing signs of crumbling. Do you:**

   a) quietly disown the venture
   b) move swiftly to the rescue
   c) wait and see what happens before making a fuss
   d) quietly analyze the position before making a decision on whether to continue?

10. **You are worried that you might begin to stammer when making a speech to an important audience. Do you:**

    a) develop a diplomatic illness
    b) tell the audience you are nervous
    c) overcome the problem by conscious effort of will
    d) during rehearsals, make yourself stammer as much as possible?

Answers overleaf.

References

1. Schlenker, B R (1980) *Impression Management*, Brooks Cole, California, p. 39.
2. See Drummond, H (1991) *Effective Decision Making*, Kogan Page, London, for an explanation of the potentially escalatory consequences of maintaining appearances.
3. Staw, B M and Ross, J (1987) 'Knowing when to pull the plug', *Harvard Business Review*, 65, pp. 68–74.

4. Hooper, J H (1948) *The Plantagenets*, Belsford, London.
5. Drummond, H (1991) 'Are good managers decisive?', *Management Decision*, forthcoming.
6. Cited in Day, R (1989) *Grand Inquisitor*, Pan Books, London.
7. Watzlawick, P, Weakland, J H, Fisch, R, (1974) *Change: Principles of Problem Formation and Resolution*, Norton, New York.
8. Korda, M (1976) *Power*, Ballantine Books, New York, p. 213.

Answers to questionnaire

1. **d.**

2. **b.**

3. **a** — sound surprised. After all the secretary usually answers. Even if you do not have a secretary, you can make it sound as if you do. D is for receptionists.

4. **c** — if you then show them in it betokens energy. If your secretary shows them in, it betokens distance — choose whichever feels appropriate.

5. **a** — you can always follow up with a memo, if you need to protect yourself in writing.

6. **d** — make people hungry for more.

7. **c** — remember, you are playing a game.

8. **a.**

9. **a** — get as far away as possible, as fast as possible.

10. **d.**

Score before reading chapter ——
Score after reading chapter   ——

5

The three basic power resources

Test your skill by answering the following questions:

1. **A colleague in another department has asked if he can second two of your least productive employees for at least three months. Do you:**

    a) say you will try and persuade them
    b) try persuasion first and resort to force if it fails
    c) instruct them to go and promise to review the position after three months
    d) instruct them to go and rejoice in having got rid of them at last?

2. **A depot is due to close. You have made three job offers to an employee who has refused all of them. Do you:**

    a) ask him what he wants
    b) ask him what is wrong with the previous three offers
    c) make one more offer and emphasize it is the last
    d) instruct him to report for work on the basis of the last offer at nine o'clock next Monday morning?

3. **You have arranged a birthday disco. At the last minute, the organizers refuse to let you use their club unless you pay an extra charge. Do you:**

    a) pay it
    b) ask him if he can afford to lose a good evening's custom
    c) run to the nearest telephone box
    d) grab the club owner by the collar and threaten him?

4. **You need to obtain an agreement to new working practices. The trade union representative says he is not prepared to discuss it until you have agreed the new overtime allowances. Do you:**

    a) insist that there can be no discussion about overtime allowances until the new working practices are agreed

    b) tell him to forget the whole thing

    c) do as he wishes as a gesture of goodwill

    d) get him to commit himself to a timetable for discussion before signing?

5. **You are running late with an exhibition. How would you approach the staff?**

    a) tell them they must stay late

    b) call for volunteers to work overtime

    c) ask them for help and give them each a souvenir afterwards

    d) ask them for help and pay them afterwards.

6. **Your organization has generated an additional profit. Unless disposed of, it will be claimed by the tax man. Do you:**

    a) use it to fund a university scholarship for employees' children

    b) hold a party for the management

    c) hold a party for management and the workforce

    d) work out how you can smuggle the cash into your private bank account?

7. **You plan to relocate your business to a new town. Which would be your priority in the first few months of operation?**

    a) managing the business

    b) becoming co-opted on to local council committees

    c) cultivating local business owners and managers

    d) getting the company logo on the railway bridge which spans the main road into town.

8. **You are the owner of a small clothing factory. What is your policy on retirement gifts?**

    a) not to bother

    b) to allow the employee to go home an hour early on their last day

    c)   to double the last wage packet
    d)   presentation of a silver needle.

9. How would you deal with an uncooperative subordinate?

    a)   take away his secretary
    b)   threaten him with the sack
    c)   reduce his performance-related pay
    d)   pay someone to put him in hospital.

10. You are the organizer of a local theatre group. Ever-precarious, the theatre has once again run into serious financial difficulties. What would be your preferred tactic for raising money?

    a)   a jumble sale
    b)   raise seat prices
    c)   see if a local industrialist will covenant a whole new theatre to be named after him.
    d)   invite locals to sponsor a seat bearing their name?

One function of power is to obtain compliance. Compliance entails motivating the power-target. Motivation requires resources either to induce or to compel. The three basic power resources are:

1. Coercion.

2. Material rewards.

3. Symbolic rewards.

Coercion encompasses both physical and mental pressure. It succeeds by eliminating the power-target's options. Material rewards means any forms of financial inducement, such as wages, bribes, bonuses, commission, and so forth. Material rewards result in calculative compliance, ie the other party obeys because they want the reward. Symbolic rewards are defined as non-financial accolades, such as badges, medals, praise and approval. Compliance is based upon the other party's need for approbation and belonging.[1]

Choice of tactics

Assuming all three resources are available in some form, then choice depends upon:

      the power-target's motivation to comply.[2,3]

Selection of the wrong power tactic can be costly and disastrous. It therefore pays to discover what motivates individuals. A hostile or cynical employee, for example, is likely to explain very precisely what you should do with your certificate, badge or medal. Likewise an employee with a modest salary, heavy mortgage and a growing family would prefer an extra increment to being nominated 'Salesman of the Year'. Conversely, monetary rewards are wasted upon highly-dedicated individuals, while coercion would destroy their motivation.

Generally speaking, symbolic reward is the most powerful and economical motivator. However, it cannot always be used, and in any case, all forms of power have advantages and disadvantages. These are discussed next.

Coercion

Coercion rests on the power-holder's ability to apply sanctions for non-compliance, such as, 'Move and I shoot', or 'Do it, or else'. The advantage of coercion is that it can be applied quickly because it requires little or no shared language with the power-target. This explains why in war, for example, the state arms itself with emergency powers enabling it to compulsorily requisition supplies and so on.

On a practical level, many managers recoil from using force because they find the idea repugnant. Certainly it can be unpleasant, but it is often easier and less distressing in the long run. For instance, when an unpopular task has to be carried out and volunteers are unavailable, it is better to say, 'Right, Peter, short straw time . . .' than to start trying to explain to Peter why he should do the job. Opt for the latter and Peter will probably tell you why Jim should do it. In the end, you will be the one who does it. This tactic is particularly effective in moving entrenched employees into another job or area. The key in all applications is to:

- emphasize that there is no alternative,
- while allowing the other party to accept the situation with dignity.

Betray any suggestion that the issue is potentially negotiable and you are lost. Equally, however, it is vital to allow the employee to retain face. This can be achieved by careful labelling of the action; for instance, a forced transfer may be called a secondment; forced resignation, ill-health retirement, and so on. Where possible, the negative should be combined with the positive, such as, 'You have done a good job at the airport these last eighteen years. I need you there, but I need you in this new role more. That is why there is no option.' Never move from that last statement. Moreover, once you have made such a decision, implement it quickly before the other person has time to rally support or create obstacles.

The risks of using force

The risk with coercion is that in seeking to remove the power-subject's alternatives:

> *it eliminates the power-holder's options too.*

Compliance results only if it is preferable to the alternatives. In that sense, the power-target actually has the final say. If the power-target opts to 'die' rather than comply, for example, the power-holder's objective is frustrated. Coercion rests upon fear; where the power-target has no fear of the power-holder, the latter is powerless.[4, 5] For instance, the prisoners whom the SS found most difficult to deal with were those from mental hospitals:

> A naked girl . . . suddenly leapt from the wagon and lay, squirming, laughing at my feet . . . . The SS men were frantic for here was something they could not understand, something that knew no order, no discipline, no obedience, no fear of violence or death.
> (Gilbert, M (1986) *The Holocaust*, Collins, London, p. 529)

Force stimulates hostility and resistance. Persuasion is therefore useless once coercion has been attempted. If force fails, the only option is to apply more, running the risk of escalation. If the power-holder is unable to apply more force, then his credibility is destroyed. Extreme coercion can also defeat its own objective by succeeding only too well. Studies of inmates of concentration camps have noted that beyond a certain point, hostility transforms into immovable apathy.[6, 7] Hostility becomes directed at other inmates, notably those of the lowest socio-economic caste and camp isolates.[8]

Maintaining control by force requires constant vigilance, and vigilance requires resources.[9] The Scots overran Hadrian's Wall as soon as the Roman guards departed. Motorists slow down when they see a police car, and speed up again as soon as the vehicle is out of sight. In management, it is possible to ensure performance standards are achieved by issuing threats and maintaining close supervision. The problem is that this is impractical on a regular basis; as soon as the manager's back is turned, everyone carries on as before.

For these reasons, if possible, force is best avoided. One of the most effective means of obtaining compliance without force is to make the other party feel in control. For example:

- 'I know you won't be pushed.'
- 'Don't feel you have too'
- 'No power on earth can force you.'
- 'The choice is yours.'

Although this tactic might appear risky, it is often very effective because it:

- removes the reason for resistance;
- forces the other party to accept responsibility.

A doctor might try and persuade a patient to undergo an operation. The more he pushes, however, the more the patient resists. A game develops whereby the patient enjoys the attention and has something to rebel against. When, however, the doctor finally says, 'OK, its your decision,' the game is over. Now the patient must take responsibility for his future.

How to apply force

Sometimes, before force can be applied it is necessary to eliminate the other party's alternatives first. This is best done:

slowly.

The secret is to move so unobtrusively that they hardly realize what you are doing until it is too late. This requires the ability to distance yourself, in order to see the end-game that you need to work towards.

The best way to proceed is to try softer options first. If these are unsuccessful force can then be justified. For example, good trade union officials are always careful to be seen to have exhausted all the stages of the grievance or negotiations procedure before resorting to industrial action.

Force requires careful planning. The miners' strikes of 1972 and 1974 succeeded because the trade union leaders had foreseen that force would be required, and had prepared their stranglehold accordingly. First, coal stocks were depleted by a long overtime ban. Next, co-operation was obtained from private mines and the dockers, who refused to handle foreign imports. Picketing was carefully organized. The timing too was deliberate, coinciding as it did with post-Christmas depression and the worst of the winter weather.

Once force is used:

- it must be applied relentlessly,[10] and
- maintained even when the other side begins to weaken.[11]

Half-measures are useless, as the other party will sense uncertainty and exploit it. In management, this means no ifs or buts. If, for example, you decide to stop supplying a company until it has paid a bill, then that resolution must be implemented without exception if it is to have any effect.

It is a mistake to ease up when the other side shows signs of weakening. Instead, pursue a seemingly contradictory policy, ie:

- maintain the pressure,
- while simultaneously showing the other party a way out.[12]

The torturers of the Spanish Inquisition, for example, always kept a confession ready by the rack for signature. Success in war demands that the victor continues to bomb the enemy while both sides talk of peace. In management, for example, the salesman must be made aware that you are in discussion with alternative suppliers, while simultaneously being told that if only certain trifling difficulties could be resolved, the contract could be signed tomorrow. (Incidentally it is better to say tomorrow rather than today. Tomorrow is soon enough to motivate, and vague enough to permit further manoeuvre.)

Countering force

Matching force with force is only an option if you are as strong as, or stronger than your opponent. Even then it is not always the most economical or effective response. It can be better to reply with:

- a gesture of aggression;
- a different kind of force;
- by turning force against itself.

Aggressive gestures

The old saying that bullies are cowards is well-founded. A basic principle of atemi jutsu, for instance, is what is known as the 'fighting spirit'. That is, a gesture of defiance suffices to signal to an aggressor that the conquest will not be quite as easy as he thought. That alone may induce him to give up. On another level, the best way to deal with peremptory communications from banks is to throw the letter on the manager's desk and say, 'How dare you send me this?' The bank will think twice about sending you such a letter again.

Countering with a different kind of force

When in 1334 the Duchess of Tyrol, Margareta Maultasch, encircled the castle of Hochosterwitz in the province of Carinthia, she knew only too well that the fortress, situated on an incredibly steep rock rising high above the valley floor, was impregnable to direct attack and would yield only to a long siege. In due course, the situation of the defenders became critical: they were down to their last ox and had only two bags of barley corn left. Margareta's situation was becoming equally pressing, albeit for different reasons: her troops were beginning to be unruly, there seemed to be no end to the siege in sight, and she had similarly urgent military business elsewhere.

(Watzlawick, P, Weakland, J H and Fisch, R (1974) *Change: Principles of Problem Formation and Resolution*, Norton, New York, p. xi)

How would you have resolved this impasse? The obvious option is to hold out for as long as possible in the hope that the other side will go away. For all the defenders knew, however, reinforcements might have been on their way. The dilemma seems unresolvable.

At this point the commandment of the castle decided upon a desperate course of action which to his men must have seemed sheer folly: he had the last ox slaughtered, had its abdominal cavity filled with the remaining barley, and ordered the carcass thrown down the steep cliff on to a meadow in front of the enemy camp. Upon receiving this scornful message from above, the discouraged Duchess abandoned the siege and moved on.

(Watzlawick, *et al.*, op. cit., p. xii)

Indirect approaches such as this work because of their capacity to achieve real change. There are two kinds of change, namely:

1. Change within a system, known as first-order change,

2. Change which actually changes the system, known as second-order change.[13]

Second-order change often seems like madness. For Gandhi, for example, to have met the British guns with passive resistance must have seemed insane. Surely they would be massacred where they sat? Yet paradoxically, Gandhi disarmed his opponents precisely because he refused to play their game. Had he attempted to fight back with guns, or sticks and stones (first-order change), his forces would indeed have been routed. By changing the terms of reference, however, he succeeded.

Likewise, before the new Licensing Act of 1976, Scotland had some of the most restrictive licensing laws and, paradoxically, some of the worst problems of drunkenness. The intuitive response would have been to exert further controls — first-order change. Proposals to lengthen opening hours seemed foolish to many people. Were matters not bad enough already? In fact, extending licensing hours affected a second-order change, by removing the real cause of the problem. Early closing times of 9.30 pm or 10 pm had prompted customers to consume vast quantities of alcohol in a short period, hence the level of drunkenness. Changing the system by relaxing the restrictions solved the problem by enabling more sensible drinking habits.

As regards achieving second-order change, the Japanese Miyamoto Musashi advises:

> If the enemy thinks of the mountains, attack like the sea: and if he thinks of the sea, attack like the mountains.
> (Musashi, M A (1989) *Book of Five Rings*, Fontana, London p. 78)

Like Gandhi, the Vietcong frustrated the Americans by refusing to give 'honest' battle. Instead they capitalized upon their own strengths ie knowledge of the terrain and the support of locals, and turned the enemy's weight against him by concentrating on ambush attacks.

This advice is valid for psychological as well as physical warfare. Violent criminals, for example, can cope with aggressive interrogation. They are helpless, however, against the policeman who says:

> Think of your mother. Is this what she brought you up for? What would she say if she saw you now? Is this what she struggled for; saved bits of her housekeeping to buy you toys: money she could have done with. Think of what you've done for her.

Such tactics are readily applicable in management situations. For example:

1. 'I work hard'.
   'It's achievement that counts.'

2. 'Your service is inefficient'
   'It's the people who use it who worry me.'

3. 'I do everything you ask.'
   'You work to the bare minimum/never seem to exercise initiative.'

Study people to identify their favorite weapons, and learn to counter. Remember, it is all a game, and sometimes a subtle one. A factory supervisor, for example, coerced by two foreign workers who replied 'Me no understand' to every instruction might have made the mistake of trying still more patient explanation. Instead, he moved the game on to his own ground by replying, 'You will when you get your wages.'

It is extremely difficult to win an argument with someone adroit at manipulating language. To compete on their terms is like stepping into the ring with a champion boxer — brave but foolish. The solution is to mount a challenge elsewhere. For example:

> This report does not address the issue. I can see nothing here that provides even the most basic analysis of the problem. I need to see the whole thing set out properly.

This could be a genuine response to a poor piece of work, or a manager looking for an excuse to procrastinate. The test is to ask, 'What is wrong with it exactly?' If the response is to repeat the previous statement, you can be sure that you are in a power game. Under no circumstances agree to rewrite the report, or you will find that it does not address the issues either. Counter such bombast with patience and detail, eg say, 'Let's go through it point by point, shall we?' Here an arch manipulator will scorn the proposal, saying it would be a waste of time as the report is irrelevant. Do not be put off; instead emphasize it is important that you understand where the deficiencies lie. Once the other person sees that their tactics have become transparent, they will begin discussing the issue sensibly.

Countering demands

Demands for concessions, and even blackmail, are common in power relations. For example, in buying a house or securing an order, it can be extremely distressing when the other party makes a demand just as the contract is about to be signed. The key to countering such force is:

- never argue with the demand,
- just stall.

To argue is to fight on the other party's terms. Instead, force them to do the running to substantiate their claim by demanding to see estimates, reports and so on. When these arrive, ask to be provided with second quotations. The other side is gambling on a panic response; unsettle them by delaying. Use the time to strengthen your position by seeking alternatives. Redress the power balance by opening or reopening negotiations. Bear in mind that the other party is probably equally anxious. Asking a blackmailer to produce his evidence and then removing it for inspection will neutralize his sting. Taking your time at this stage may even reverse the situation completely, as the other party begins to worry about completing the transaction. Is the vendor of the property, for example, really prepared to put the house back on the market again? Having demanded concessions he may now start offering them in order to regain your interest.

Turning force against itself

This means using your opponent's strength to his own disadvantage. Watlawick *et al.* recount an excellent example of this technique. The case concerns the Nazi persecution of Jews in Denmark. When the Jews were ordered to wear yellow stars, the King of Denmark replied to Nazi officials that, since everyone in his country was equal, everyone would wear a yellow star.[14]

Likewise, politicians who threaten to resign from the Cabinet in order to force their own way over an issue base their power on fears about rumours of division within the government. This strength, however, can be used against them by accepting their resignation. This tactic simultaneously solves any problem of a split in government, as the source of the division is then no longer part of it.

Innumerable possibilities exist for applying this technique in organizations. A company's high public profile can be used against it by threats of exposure. An organization which prides itself upon risk-taking may be led to destruction by over-adventurous speculation.

At the individual level, someone who is extremely conscientious and painstaking can be damned as slow and unimaginative. Conversely, someone whose output is high is vulnerable to accusations of shallowness or carelessness. Qualities of resolve and determination can be turned against someone by involving them in a losing course of action. In those circumstances, their strengths become weaknesses, as they ensure persistence when all objective criteria clearly dictate withdrawal.[15]

Coping with acute coercion

The foregoing tactics require time and thought for successful deployment.

They are therefore of limited value *in extremis*. In these circumstances, coercion succeeds through a combination of:

- emotional upset;
- fear.

People suddenly experiencing high levels of fear and upset are prone to behaving:

- out of character;
- against their own interests.

In such circumstances, people will sign confessions of murder even though they are innocent. This explains why initial statements are often retracted, ie once someone has calmed down it is possible for them to explain matters.[16] The problem then, of course, is that their credibility may be damaged irreparably.[17]

If faced with severe pressure, be extremely circumspect about what you say or do, and never:

- admit blame;
- try and explain yourself;
- commit yourself.

It is essential to withdraw and to take time to compose yourself. Do not let anyone push you. Respond only when you feel ready and able to do so. Incidentally, if the incident has disciplinary implications, it is legally unfair to conduct any interview or enquiry unless the employee is fit to participate.[18]

Reward

'What's in it for me?'

Rewards are powerful motivators. They can be used to improve the quality of service and attention in most walks of life, and are even capable of stimulating sublime effort and performance. Generally speaking:

the more rewarding you are, the more power you possess.

Again, power exists at the margin. Many people forget this when dealing with others, and so fail to realize the full potential of a situation. For instance, it may be someone's job to take a message. Just saying, 'Thank-you, you have been most helpful,' is a reward. Not only does it increase the likelihood of the message being delivered, but it creates a good foundation for the future, as people actively seek to please those who reward them.

Rewards, like any other form of power, need not be real for them to be effective. All that matters is that the power target believes in the power-holder's capability and intention to gratify him. It is therefore possible to manipulate people by promises. The most powerful promises are those which dangle the distant, but non-too-distant prospect of reward. Fulfilment is invariably postponed and postponed again until the power-holder's purpose is served.

Effective rewards are those which the other party values. It is point-less, for instance, to buy someone an expensive shirt as a present if they cannot afford an outfit to match. Bear in mind that resources you take for granted may be highly prized by someone else. Accordingly, the best form of reward is one which is:

- cheap to you;
- valuable to the other person.[19]

Traders and professionals, for example, will gladly serve a prestigious client free of charge because of all the other business emanating from the association. Likewise, the derelict land attached to your house may be an eyesore to you, yet sought after as a parking space by a neighbour. In pay bargaining, the trade unions may be willing to forgo part of a monetary claim in return for an extension of flexi-time provisions. This costs management very little yet represents a significant gain to the other side. A good point for power-seekers to remember is:

why give anything away when you can get something for it?

Monetary power

A colleague of mine once kept hens. While ever he gave away the odd half-dozen eggs to office staff, all was well. Everything changed, how-ever, when he started to sell his produce. People who had been pre-viously grateful now found that their eggs were too small; the shell was the wrong colour, the yolks were dreary, and so on. A pleasurable hobby fast became a source of rancour. The moral of this tale is:

you get only what you pay for.

This is because compliance is basically calculative.[20] This means that the power-subject's sole motivation is to obtain the reward. Mercenary soldiers, for example, fight only for as long as they are paid. Blue collar workers will only do extra in return for overtime rates.

Calculative compliance affects the relationship between the power-holder and the power-target. Prostitutes, for instance, generally resent clients. If the rewards are perceived as inequitable, hostility results. Moreover, if rewards are administered regularly, they come to be experienced as coercion.[21] Commission payments, for example, are primarily intended to motivate. The power-subject, however, may perceive them as a dread measure of performance. Likewise, rewarding a schoolchild for exam results is double-edged, in that past achievements form a benchmark for future expectations.

Managing calculative compliance

Despite its limitations, material reward has considerable power to move. The reason that book clubs, for example, continue to use advertisements styled 'Three for only a pound' is that they work. Old and unimaginative they may be, but are extremely effective. Their effectiveness lies in their appeal to greed. Greed is hypnotic — respondents see only the carrot, and not the costs of accepting it. Careful management, however, is essential to maintain control and optimize the possibilities.

The implications of calculative compliance for power-holders are:

1. Do not be deceived by friendliness.

2. If your hand is empty, never reveal it.

3. Ensure delivery precedes reward.

4. Always trade upon assets, never give them away.

5. An appeal to greed seldom fails.

Remember:

> *The dog wags his tail for the biscuit, not for you.*
> (Spanish proverb)

When people want something, they ingratiate themselves with whoever has the power to give. It is easy to deceive oneself into believing that supplicants like you, and that they will behave loyally and reciprocate favours and assistance. The reality is, they are probably secretly bitter. What is certain is that:

> *as soon as they have what they want, they will desert you.*

Those who can no longer reward, no longer have power. Consequently, it is in the power-holder's interests to keep others dangling on the basis of a promise for as long as possible. Once rewards are distributed, maintain control by appealing to greed, ie the promise of more.

Never reward in anticipation of performance, or to placate someone. If you do, all that will happen is that the other party will say, 'thank you very much', and forget about his side of the bargain. Incidentally, if another person wants something from you:

use it to get something in return.

Pitching the reward

Too big a reward is as bad as one that is too small. People seldom appreciate anything which they:

- perceive as unearned;[22] or
- cannot reciprocate.

On the first point, rewards should always be proportional to effort and performance, otherwise they lose their effect as the power-subject is no longer able to relate the two. By all means deliver more than you promise, but keep it within the ratio.

On the second point, the issues are finally balanced. Take a business colleague for a cheap lunch and he may feel insulted. On the other hand, taking him for an expensive one may make him feel embarrassed if he is expected to return hospitality. The choice depends upon the desired relationship with the other party. If the sole objective is to create and emphasize power, then be lavish and pick up the bill. If the aim is to create a sound personal or working relationship, combine generosity and restraint. For example, make it an excellent pub-lunch, or a luxurious afternoon tea.

Avoid being manipulated

Beware vague mellifluous statements such as, 'You could be a candidate for promotion in two or three years.' Such sentiments are intended to keep you dangling while others advance themselves. The test for sincerity is whether deeds match words. Engagement rings, for instance, originally served as a pledge of good faith until the marriage contract could be executed. Believe in fine words only if they are underwritten by something substantial. Be particularly suspicious if distant prospects are contingent upon efforts and/or sacrifices in the present.

The power of symbolic reward

Why money is not everything

Symbols are potentially more potent than material rewards. This is because their strength derives from the power-subject's needs for:

- esteem;
- affiliation;
- belonging.[23]

According to Maslow, once basic needs for food, shelter and material comfort are satisfied, these so-called 'higher-order needs' predominate.[24] Fulfilment of these higher-order needs explains why people devote time to unpaid activities and accept jobs which offer low pay but high personal satisfaction.

As explained at the beginning of this chapter, coercion and monetary rewards are incapable of stimulating or sustaining highly-committed individuals. The most apposite reward is one which signifies approbation. For example, I have known blue collar staff help erect a sports stand in return for a promotional T-shirt — yet they would have refused to do the work on an overtime basis. This is because voluntary participation satisfied their esteem and belonging needs, enabling them to identify personally with the charity event, rather than as hired hands. The T-shirt cemented these feelings, whereas money would not have done.

This explains why voluntary organizations are careful to develop a system of accolades such as certificates, medals for long service, and awards for distinguished service. The military, too, utilize symbolic power through campaign medals, awards for bravery, and the like.

Rewarding people need not always require huge resources. The easiest symbols to manipulate, and often the most valued are:

- praise;
- appreciation;
- attention.

Approbation should never be continuous, otherwise the other party will become suspicious. The only exceptions to this rule are those who are really hostile and provocative. Management of such individuals requires over-compensation with praise. Never, however, reward bad behaviour, even with anger, as any form of attention can represent gratification.

Symbols can also be used to control behaviour, by making a person feel involved and important. Mothers are always advised to ensure that when a second child is born, the first feels needed by getting to help with the new baby and then being rewarded with special attention. Adults are little different.

Keep money out

It is a mistake to offer money to people who genuinely wish to help. A householder who gave shelter and hospitality to picketing miners would have had a completely different relationship with them had he accepted payment. The miners would have seen him as profiting from them. Instead, he was subsequently presented with a miner's lamp.

Accolades and money should be kept well apart. The reason awards such as 'Sales Person of the Year' incur cynicism and derision is they are too closely linked with profits and other monetary considerations. Accolades work best over issues which have strong emotional appeal, such as safety, education and training, where presentations and awards ceremonies emphasize commitment.

Symbolic gestures

Symbolic gestures have great power to move. At the end of the Remembrance Day service in the Albert Hall, the poppies fall, one for every life lost. Everyone present is touched, literally. This is a much more poignant act than publishing figures and other statistical data. Symbolism is equally powerful in reverse. Michael Foot, the former leader of the Labour Party, lost support by appearing at the Cenotaph in an old duffel coat. Ex-service men were insulted because, as they saw it, Foot put his own convenience or ideology above respect for the dead.

Symbols, luck and prosperity

Symbols can create faith. Faith is power because it persuades individuals that they can accomplish their goals for good or for ill. Coats of arms, for example, often symbolize a turn of fortune. A baron who saved his king from being savaged by a wild boar, for instance, would have been raised to an earldom. The boar might then be commemorated in his coat of arms as a symbol of luck. Similarly, I know of a most successful entrepreneur who deliberately empowered himself by creating his company's name from the names of people who had helped in its formation. This phenomenon works in reverse, for instance the superstition surrounding the ravens of the Tower of London and Halley's comet.

Symbols can be manipulated to influence others. When William the Conqueror fell on the beach at Hastings, his followers saw it as an ominous sign. William, however, reversed their feelings by proclaiming that he had seized England in his hands.

In organizations, it is possible to deliberately create and emphasize symbols of hope or despair. People tend to be most susceptible in times of great uncertainty. The simplest example is the project labelled as having gone right or wrong from the start. Likewise, if the weather is wet it may be possible to put heart into a visitor by saying: 'You bring the refreshing waters of change'; if the weather happens to be dry, say 'The sun shines upon us.' Arranging for the clock to crash down from the wall, or the windows to fly open eerily at a critical juncture, requires more effort but may be worthwhile as it is surprising just how superstitious many people are!

Using accolades to make money

Symbols can be used to make money, particularly if they grant a form of immortality in return.[25] Charities have long exploited this, by enabling people or organizations to perpetuate their name by endowing gifts. Universities too have attracted large endowments by naming professorships and lectureships after individuals or organizations. On a much smaller scale, zoos have obtained funds by inviting the public to sponsor an animal, while theatres have raised money by allowing sponsors to carve their name on a slate as part of a roof-renewal scheme. Likewise, companies give their services free in an emergency, in order to profit from the publicity.

'They shall not pass'

It is important to appreciate that nations, groups and individuals will fight for what is symbolically important, regardless of its strategic importance, or whether such defence is actually counter-productive. The French defence of the fortress of Verdun in the First World War, is one such example.

Sensitivity to such sentiments pays dividends. For example, it is essential to take them into account when trying to achieve change. A trade union which has emphasized its committment to a 'no compulsory redundancies' policy, for instance, must be handled very carefully if drastic staff reductions are required. Alternatively, it may be in the power-seeker's interests to deliberately emphasize such sentiments, in order to generate resistance.

Symbolic coercion

The negative use of symbols is often regarded by recipients as a worse punishment than disciplinary action or monetary penalty. Moving someone from a private office into an open-plan space, for example, or excluding them from the management team, deprives them of esteem and a sense of belonging. Shame, ridicule and exclusion can hurt much more than economic deprivation such as a fine, for example, as they affect esteem and belonging needs. For that reason, such sanctions incur the heaviest resistance.

Sensitivity is important even where change does not imply criticism. Reorganization of a city's market structure, for example, was delayed for months because one employee opposed it. It emerged that the sole reason for his intransigence was that under the new arrangements, he would no longer wear a uniform. Once this was understood, his jacket, decked in gold braid and bearing the title 'Inspector', was immediately restored to him.

The most ordinary objects can possess great symbolic importance. I once knew of an employee who secured for himself an extra table in an open-plan office. The table came to symbolize his seniority, and woe betide anyone who cast a covetous eye upon it.

Something for Nothing

Symbols can be used to facilitate change. It is surprising sometimes what people will do for a designated place in the car park, or to become entitled to first-class rail travel. Post titles too can be manipulated; for example, redesignating assistant managers as managers: the head typist as registrar, head of finance as director of finance, and so on.

Guard against over-selling. A carpet salesman is a carpet salesman. Calling him a design consultant only leads customers to distrust both the bearer of the title and the organization which gave him it.

Summary

- The three basic resources which can be used to obtain compliance are coercion, material reward, and symbolic reward.

- Selection of tactic depends upon the power-target's motivation to comply.

- Coercion works by eliminating the power-target's options.

- The problem with coercion is that it eliminates the power-holder's options too.

- Persuasion is useless once force has been attempted.

- Force requires vigilance, to maintain it.

- Paradoxically, removal of force can result in compliance.

- In most situations, force is best applied slowly, and as a last resort.

- Once force is used, it must be used to the full.

- When the other party begins to weaken it is essential to maintain the pressure, while simultaneously showing him a way out.

- If you are weaker than your opponent, never reply with force. Instead try:
  - a gesture of aggression;
  - a different kind of force; or
  - turning force against itself.

- Never commit yourself to anything while feeling distressed or frightened, as you are likely to behave out of character and against your own interests.

- Rewarding people are attractive and therefore powerful.

- An effective reward is something the recipient values.

- Where money is involved, you only get what you pay for.

- If used regularly, rewards can be experienced as coercion.

- Rewards buy only ingratiation — never loyalty or gratitude. People often secretly resent those who have the power to reward them.

- Capitalize on all of your assets. If someone wants something from you, let them pay for it.

- An appeal to greed seldom fails.

- People seldom appreciate rewards which they perceive as unearned, or cannot reciprocate.

- Never allow yourself to be manipulated by vague, honeyed promises.

- Symbols are more potent than monetary rewards when recipients seek higher need fulfilment.

- Examples of symbolic rewards include badges, medals, certificates, and not least, praise, appreciation and attention.

- It is a mistake to pay people who wish to help.

- Accolades and money should be kept separate.

- Symbols have great power to move and create faith, for good or for bad.

- Symbols can be used to make money.

- People fight hardest for what is symbolically important to them.

- Symbols can be used to facilitate change, such as giving someone a more prestigious job title.

USING POWER QUESTIONNAIRE

Having read the chapter re-test yourself:

1. **A colleague in another department has asked if he can second two of your least productive employees for at least three months. Do you:**

   a) say you will try and persuade them
   b) try persuasion first and resort to force if it fails
   c) instruct them to go temporarily, and promise to review the position after three months
   d) instruct them to go, and rejoice in having got rid of them at last?

2. **A depot is due to close. You have made three job offers to an employee, who has refused all of them. Do you:**

   a) ask him what he wants
   b) ask him what is wrong with the previous three offers
   c) make one more offer and emphasize it is the last
   d) instruct him to report for work on the basis of the last offer at nine o'clock next Monday morning?

3. **You have arranged a birthday disco. At the last minute the owners refuse to allow exclusive use of the club unless you pay an extra charge. Do you:**

   a) pay it
   b) ask him if he can afford to lose an evening's custom
   c) run to the nearest telephone box
   d) grab the club owner by the collar and threaten him?

4. **You need to obtain an agreement to new working practices. The trade union representative says he is not prepared to discuss it until you have agreed the new overtime allowances. Do you:**

   a) insist that there can be no discussion about overtime allowances until the new working practices are agreed
   b) tell him to forget the whole thing
   c) do as he wishes as a gesture of goodwill
   d) get him to commit himself to a timetable for discussion before signing?

5. **You are running late with an exhibition. How would you approach the staff?**

   a) tell them they must stay late
   b) call for volunteers to work overtime
   c) ask them for help and give them each a souvenir afterwards
   d) ask them for help and pay them afterwards?

6. **Your organization has generated an additional profit. Unless disposed of, it will be claimed by the tax man. Do you:**

   a) use it to fund a university scholarship for employee's children
   b) hold a party for the management
   c) hold a party for management and the workforce
   d) work out how you can smuggle the cash into your private bank account?

7. **You plan to relocate your business to a new town. Which would be your priority in the first few months of operation?**

   a) managing the business
   b) becoming co-opted on to local council committees
   c) cultivating local business owners and managers
   d) getting the company logo on the railway bridge which spans the main road into town.

8. **You are the owner of a small clothing factory. What is your policy on retirement gifts?**

   a) not to bother
   b) to allow the employee to go home an hour early on their last day
   c) to double the last wage packet
   d) presentation of a silver needle.

9. **How would you deal with an uncooperative subordinate?**

   a) take away his secretary
   b) threaten him with the sack
   c) reduce his performance-related pay
   d) pay someone to put him in hospital.

10. **You are the organizer of a local theatre group. Ever-precarious, the theatre has once again run into serious**

financial difficulties. What would be your preferred tactic for raising money?

a) a jumble sale
b) raise seat prices
c) see if a local industrialist will covenant a whole new theatre to be named after him
d) invite locals to sponsor a seat bearing their name.

Answers overleaf.

References

1. Etzioni, A (1975) *A Comparative Analysis of Complex Organizations*, Collier Macmillan, London.
2. Etzioni, op. cit.
3. Wrong, D H (1979) *Power: Its Forms Bases and Uses*, Basil Blackwell, Oxford.
4. Ng, S H (1980), *The Social Psychology of Power*, Academic Press, London.
5. Bacharach, P and Baratz, M S (1970) *Power and Poverty: Theory and Practice*, Oxford University Press, New York.
6. Bettleheim, B 'Individual and mass behaviour in extreme situations', *Journal of Abnormal and Social Psychology*, 1943, 38, pp. 417–52.
7. Bloch, H A 'The personality of inmates of concentration camps', *American Journal of Sociology*, 1947, 52, pp. 335–41.
8. Cohen, E A (1953) *Human Endeavour in Concentration Camps*, Hook Norton, New York.
9. Wrong, op. cit.
10. Gilbert, M (1983) *Finest Hour: Winston S. Churchill 1939–41*, Heinemann, London.
11. Kissinger, H (1979) *The White House Years*, Weidenfeld & Nicholson and Michael Joseph, London.
12. Kissinger, op. cit.
13. Watzlawick, P Weakland, J H and Fisch, R (1974), *Change: Principles of Problem Formation and Resolution*, Norton, New York, p xi.
14. Watzlawick, *et al.* op. cit.
15. Staw, B M and Ross, J (1987) 'Behavior in escalation situations: antecedents, prototypes and solutions.' In *Research in Organization Behavior*, JAI Press, London, 9, pp. 39–78.
16. Sargant, W (1957) *Battle for the Mind*, Heinemann, London.
17. Tennyson-Jesse, F (1957) *Trials of Timothy John Evans and John Reginald Halliday Christie*, Wm. Hodge, London.
18. Drummond, H (1990) *Managing Difficult Staff*, Kogan Page, London.
19. Fisher, R and Ury, W (1983) *Getting to Yes*, Hutchinson, London.

20. Etzioni, op. cit.
21. Wrong, op. cit.
22. Adams, J S 'Inequity in Social Exchange'. In L Berkowitz (ed) (1965), *Advances in Experimental Psychology*, Academic Press, New York.
23. Etzioni, op. cit.
24. Maslow, A H (1954) *Motivation and Personality*, Harper & Brother, New York.
25. Ng, op. cit.

Answers to questionnaire

1. **c** — it solves the problem, and allows the individuals to retain dignity without committing you to anything

2. **d** — the employee is playing games. You have done all that can be reasonably expected. There is no point in continuing to make offers to people who keep refusing them.

3. **b** — they are trying to take you for a ride. If the place is booked for the evening, who else is going to occupy it at this late stage? D is language they will understand, but not advisable.

4. **a.**

5. **c.**

6. **a** — you will feel good about it forever.

7. **d** — you need to show yourself and the world that you have arrived. The others are all important however, especially a. Neglect it and the logo will be there long after you have gone.

8. **d** — c would make a nice addition. Man cannot live on bread alone, but a spare loaf comes in handy.

9. **a** — you should of course discuss his performance, but there are other ways of helping people move on.

10. **c** — simplifies everything if it can be done. Failing that, try d.

Score before reading chapter: ——

Score after reading chapter: ——

6
Knowledge as power

Test yourself by answering the following questions:

1. **You are in negotiations with a company. Which of the following would interest you most?**

   a) the annual report
   b) an accountant's confidential report
   c) the merchant banker's correspondence file
   d) the chief executive's private diary.

2. **Your boss has a new secretary. Do you:**

   a) ask lots of questions
   b) ask how on earth he puts up with things
   c) say how much better organized the boss seems
   d) ask if he has any problems?

3. **You hear angry voices as you approach a door. Do you?**

   a) cough loudly
   b) pause and listen
   c) turn away
   d) walk straight in?

4. **A car you bought nine months ago is fast becoming a liability. Do you:**

   a) keep repairing it
   b) take it back to the garage and complain
   c) take it back to the garage and say you are getting bored with it

d) explain to the garage that you are looking for something more expensive, as you have come into money?

5. **Which of the following do you carry?**

a) personal organizer and pen
b) pocket calculator
c) hand-held dictating machine
d) telephone recording attachment for hand-held machine.

6. **When transacting business or making enquiries, do you make notes of telephone conversations:**

a) always
b) sometimes
c) rarely
d) never?

7. **An interesting job is advertised, with a telephone contact for enquiries. Do you:**

a) wait and see if you are shortlisted
b) pick up the phone at once
c) use it as an opportunity to sell yourself
d) jot down a few questions and then telephone?

8. **You are late for a meeting. Do you:**

a) go straight there
b) call at your office for the papers
c) get your secretary to telephone and say you will be along in twenty minutes
d) cancel?

9. **You are meeting a new contractor for the first time. Do you:**

a) take detailed notes during the meeting
b) concentrate on listening, but write down key points afterwards
c) ask your secretary to take notes
d) hide a tape recorder in the room?

10. **You discover that a plant which you had said was running at a serious loss is in fact returning a healthy profit. The mistake is due to inefficiencies within your own department. Do you:**

a) rush out and spread the good news
b) explain that new information has come to light which may show the position is not as bad as feared
c) say nothing but modify the accounts gradually
d) say nothing and let everyone continue to believe that the plant is losing money?

Information is power because:

- it reduces uncertainty;
- it gives power-seekers the potential to manipulate others;
- it may enable the weak to defeat the strong.

In power relations, incomplete information is inevitable. Success depends upon achieving a margin of superiority by exploiting existing sources, through being:

- curious;
- industrious;
- quiet;
- patient;
- vigilant;
- close.

Each of these is now discussed in turn.

The power of curiosity

Einstein is said to have attributed his success to curiosity. Curiosity is vital in intelligence-gathering, because it leads to discovery. Allow your sense of curiosity freedom; where it leads, follow.

The power of your own job knowledge should not be under-estimated, however lowly your role. It has been suggested, for example, that for centuries the Chinese civil service was dominated by its clerks, as they alone knew the workings of the bureaucracy.[1] Likewise, junior staff may know that a senior manager is about to be ousted long before anyone else, through being asked to obtain an estimate of the latter's pension benefits.

Information which routinely passes through your hands is a source of power, because others do not have access to it. Glancing through files, noting the odd invoice, perusing letters and so on, is time well spent. Even if the information means nothing now, one day it could be significant. A policy officer, for example, once scribbled on a form: 'It is essential we employ a black person.' The personnel officer, who disliked the policy officer, noted the comment. The appointee was incompetent. An enquiry was held and the form was used to prove that the policy officer had committed a serious breach of discipline by discriminating illegally in making the appointment.

It is possible, of course, to obtain access to data without authority. Information has to be stored somewhere, thus rendering it vulnerable to a little gentle espionage. Few offices are properly secure. In fact, it is amazing to see the amount of confidential information left lying on desks or placed in unlocked drawers and cabinets. A regular stroll round the building after home-time can yield dividends. One curious tug at a filing cabinet may reveal a treasure trove, which can then be re-visited periodically. Word processors may yield secrets at the mere touch of a button. Computer discs may repay discreet copying. Avoid being caught out yourself, however. There are people who will go to enormous lengths to obtain information. The author has known employees make regular and systematic searches of other people's offices — including the waste-paper bin, notepads, loose sheets, blotting pads, doodle pads, desk drawers and so on. Distasteful though it may sound, it happens — so beware.

Useful industry

Much information is in any case there for the taking by those willing to expend the necessary time and effort. For example:

> Two managers, A and B, were in dispute over the allocation of newly-vacated floorspace. Both managers claimed that their staff were working in cramped conditions. The group manager called the two managers to a meeting to discuss the problem. Manager A arrived ready to browbeat in order to get what he wanted. As soon as the meeting started, Manager A declaimed the lack of space; said how his staff were complaining, and insisted he must have the extra room.

If you were manager B, how would you have responded?

> Manager B did not argue. Instead he produced two floor-plans. These showed that manager A's staff already occupied twice the amount of floor space as manager B's.

Who do you imagine won the argument? As this case shows, knowledge is indeed power, but only if you are prepared to seek it out.

Most of us carry a great deal of knowledge around with us in our heads. We often forgo any benefit from it, however, because we fail to draw inferences from it. This is a pity, because knowledge can enable us to predict the behaviour of others.[2] Compare, for example, these two biographical profiles:

PROFILE A

Age: 44

Formal qualifications: 5 O levels

Current post:	Financial Controller	
Previous posts:	Senior Finance Officer	7 Years
	Finance Officer	4 Years
	Section Leader	3 Years
	Senior Clerk	8 Years
	Clerk	6 Years

PROFILE B

Age: 33

Qualifications: B.Sc. MBA Membership of Chartered Institute of Builders

Current post: General Manager

Previous appointments	Deputy General Manager	2 Years
	Works Manager	2 Years
	Site Manager	4 Years
	Assistant Site Manager	2 Years
	Cost and Management Accounts Officer	2 Years

If under threat, which of these two individuals is likely to fight hardest for his corner? The subject of Profile A holds a professional job without any formal qualifications. His career pattern suggests he has worked his way up from the bottom of the organization. Given that he probably had ample opportunity to acquire qualifications, why has he not done so? Or has he tried and failed? Might this suggest a serious scholastic deficiency? If so, he probably compensates for it by being highly streetwise. His career options are probably extremely limited, as his lack of qualifications and somewhat pedestrian experience is likely to debar him from being shortlisted for jobs in other organizations.

The subject of Profile B is potentially much more marketable. With one exception, the maximum time spent in any one job has been two years. He is therefore less likely to fight to retain his job than the other manager, because he knows he can easily find a job elsewhere. The other manager must cling to what he has and is likely to use his street skills to the point of unscrupulousness.

Much, too, can be deduced from fragments of knowledge. For example, a chief accountant has a problem with one of his accountants, someone with a schoolboy face and large ears. Technically the accountant's work is very good: he is intelligent and hard working. However, his relations with other staff are poor, as they find him sarcastic and over-bearing. The chief accountant is also conscious of a less than respectful attitude towards himself. A glance at the accountant's personal file reveals the A levels and grades:

Chemistry   D
Physics   B
Biology   B

The combination of subjects immediately suggests someone with aspirations to become a doctor. The grade D in chemistry probably cost him a place in medical school. If this is correct, it explains why he is ill-adjusted to his present role and why he vents his frustration on others. He is probably angry and unhappy.

Why silence is golden

People generally prefer talking to listening. Power-seekers do the opposite: ie they:

- reveal as little as possible about themselves:
- concentrate upon listening and asking questions.

The less the other party knows about you and the more you know about them, the better. In talking, information is imparted. People, including those who should know better, can be very indiscreet. For instance:

ESTATE AGENT:	22 Lavender Cottages. Yes it's just come back on the market. The only thing wrong with it is that the cellar needs some special damp-proofing, which the vendor is willing to pay for.
PURCHASER:	Is it vacant?
ESTATE AGENT:	Yes, the vendor got made redundant so he took a job in Ireland.
PURCHASER:	Well I'll take a look at it, but it seems a bit expensive for what it is.
ESTATE AGENT:	I think the vendor might take an offer.

Look at what this casual conversation reveals. The estate agent discloses that one sale has already failed, and that the vendor is now living far from home. This suggests that the vendor may be becoming anxious to be relieved of the responsibility for the property and to realize the proceeds from the sale. Furthermore, the estate agent commits the vendor to paying for repairs which the purchaser might have been prepared to fund. Worst, the estate agent then divulges that the asking price is inflated.

In fact, the purchaser was desperate to acquire the property, and would have paid more than the purchase price for it. His circumspection plus the estate agent's careless talk saved him £7,000. Remember, in power relations, the objective is to do a little better than you otherwise might. Right now, what could you do with £7,000?

It is important to say something about yourself in order to build trust and make the other party feel comfortable with you. Plan in advance what you will disclose. The best advice is to stick to generalities. Above all:

never reveal the pressure you are under.

If you let the other party see that you must do a deal, ie that you have fallen in love with the property, that the bank manager is hounding you, that you are about to be made redundant and have no other job offers, and so on, they will use the information against you.

The power of patience

Although it is important to probe, sometimes more can be gleaned by not asking. If someone starts talking, avoid interrupting; you can always ask questions later. If someone reveals something significant, try not to betray interest — otherwise they may realize they have been indiscreet, and clam up.

This particularly applies to secretaries. Secretaries are invariably worth cultivating. They tend to operate in a network, trading information with other secretaries. If anyone knows who is drinking a bottle of whisky a day, whose stars are in the ascendant and vice versa, they do. Never press for information. Just be polite, friendly, stop for a chat, build a relationship and keep listening. You will be astonished at what eventually pours forth. Once a degree of rapport is established, some safe ways of stimulating the information flow are:

1. Is the boss in?

This can result in his whereabouts for the next two weeks being revealed. It's always useful to know what people are up to.

2. What sort of mood is he in?

If the boss is under pressure, this is the way to find out who is wielding the knives, and with what effect.

3. Is it worth risking . . . , what do you think?

Although this question seldom reveals information, it flatters the secretary's sense of power. Flattery is powerfully conducive to revealing confidences. New secretaries, incidentally, will be mollified to learn how much better organized things are, and how the boss has become easier to cope with, since their arrival.

4. How's things?

This is a cue to vent exasperation. It usually produces the latest news.

If you have a secretary you can be sure that she will trade information about you. Counter by giving the appearance of mutual trust and confidence, while simultaneously observing the wisdom of the fool — say less than thou knowest — always.

The power of vigilance

As crime takes place all around, it follows that the clues to crime in progress are also all around. Successful policeman are usually:

- observant;
- quick to interpret observations.

A car with its windscreen wipers on for more than a few seconds in dry weather suggests that the driver is unfamiliar with the controls and may perhaps indicate that the vehicle has been stolen. A cheap number-plate crudely attached to an expensive car is similarly suspicious.[3]

Clues likewise exist everywhere in organizations. Moreover they are often more reliable than human testimony.[4] Someone who regularly has bags under his eyes, or whose hands shake, for example, is under strain, whatever he might say. A senior manager doing his own photocopying can be extremely significant; it may suggest something so sensitive afoot that not even the secretary is trusted. (Incidentally, see if you can find those sheets; one might even have been left in the photocopier.) Likewise, observe the demeanour of those around you. At the onset of the Cuban Missile crisis, for instance, facial expressions accurately reflected which officials knew about the missiles, and which ones did not.[5] A sudden increase in the number of meetings; an upsurge in to-ings and fro-ings, people burying themselves in their offices, huddling in groups, all signal a crisis.

On a more mundane level it can pay to be alert for signs of changes in mood. Discover the barometers, and watch them. Simple things like door open or door closed can signal whether someone wishes to be disturbed or not. Choice of suit can signal the perceived importance of a meeting. Even choice of pen may be significant. I knew of one manager who alternated between biro and fountain pen. The former signified brash and busy, whereas the latter signified a contemplative mood. To get something signed quickly, it was best to approach on a biro-wielding day. To engage him in discussion it was best to wait until the fountain pen appeared. Such are the simple factors which can determine success or failure.

It is important to know about organizational cliques and cabals. A lunch-time visit to local pubs is a most effective means of discovering who talks to whom. Note, however, that people who socialize together do not necessarily like one another. Many alliances are born of fear. Knowledge of darker emotions can be manipulated to advantage. A junior manager, for example, wanted a photocopier. He knew the director of administration was against buying photocopiers. However, the financial controller held the money, and the financial controller did not like the director of administration. The junior manager knew this, and so submitted his request to the financial controller in the hope that he might authorize the purchase to provoke his colleague. Three days later, the photocopier arrived.

Getting close

The Romans used to say, to assassinate someone, first get close to them. Closeness yields information, as trust are deposited and weaknesses gleaned. Walking through an open-plan office with eyes and ears open is a form of closeness. The more you do it, the better. There is evidence that managers attach more credence to information supplied by those they see frequently than those they see infrequently.[6] This of course means that the staff most likely to be undermining you are not the overtly hostile or uncooperative, but those smiling, ever-gracious individuals whom you would least suspect of treachery.

Creating your own database

Knowledge is power only if it can be recalled and deployed when needed. Most people forget most of what they ever learn. How often, for example, have you failed to make a point at a meeting, for want of a vital piece of information? Chance, remember, favours the prepared. You must be ready to capitalize upon luck by creating and managing your own database. This means:

1. Recording potentially significant information.

2. Being able to recall with ease what you have recorded.

3. Being able to make computations and cross-comparisons with ease.

Power and success derive from doing that little bit more than everyone else. The first step is to acquire the habit of note-taking. If you discover an interesting piece of information, or hold a potentially important conversation, record it. The most important time for note-taking is:

- at the start of a venture;
- when meeting someone for the first time.

People are often forthcoming early on in a project, or when meeting someone new, because they do not immediately realize the intentions of the other party. Consequently, bargaining often starts long before one party is aware of what is happening. For example, the moment you enter a car showroom, a game is in progress. The salesman who appears to be working on a sheet of figures is probably watching you and listening to you intently. Likewise, someone engaging you in casual conversation may be doing so because they intend to apply for a vacancy due to arise in your department.

First impressions are always worth recording. It is surprising the amount people will reveal in casual conversation. Once they realize that you want something, however, they are more likely to be circumspect about what they say and how they behave.

The rewards of note-taking are out of all proportion to the time required. A senior partner of a firm of consultants, for instance, once intimated to a freelance consultant that his company relied heavily upon subcontracting work. The consultant noted the point. Two months later, the senior partner sought to engage the freelance consultant. During the negotiations over fees, the senior partner tried to lower the consultant's expectations by saying that he seldom engaged freelancers, thus implying that he was doing the latter a favour in finding work for him. The senior partner was deservedly embarrassed when the consultant recounted their previous conversation almost verbatim. Likewise, during initial discussions on a house purchase, an estate agent casually mentioned a crack in the wall. This highly significant piece of information might have been lost amid all the other details about room sizes, carpets, curtains and so on, had the purchaser not made a note of it.

Self management

An important but frequently neglected database is your own self. It pays to record and review periodically:

1. What you are doing and why.

2. What has and has not been achieved.

3. Reservations and worst fears.

The mere act of committing such details to paper creates power, because it provides a basis for planning and evaluation.[7] Furthermore, it creates an edge over individuals who merely drift along, never perceiving the long-term consequences of seemingly innocuous decisions until it is too late.[8, 9]

Essential equipment

This comprises:

1. A notebook with pen and calculator

This may sound obvious, but as the Scottish saying goes, 'The things you see when you dinnae have a gun.' Personal organizers are an effective form of notebook, because they can function as mini-data-bases, enabling fast recall of addresses, notes, ideas and, not least, cross-comparisons. Having everything in one place enables you to recognize connections; to calculate the implications of an offer as you speak on the telephone, and so on.

The importance of speed cannot be over-emphasized. A calculator, for example, enables claims made by others at meetings to be checked there and then while the item is at the forefront of attention and before decisions are made. Hand-held computers are a potential substitute.

2. A hand-held dictating machine

These are very useful for making notes quickly and recording telephone conversations. Note, however, that it is illegal to record a conversation without the other party's knowledge.

3. A carefully thought-out, properly maintained filing and cross-referencing system

The most careful recording and reading are a waste of time unless you can:

a) recall information;
b) retrieve it.

An office should ideally function as a database. Yet many managers are unaware of what information they possess, or where to find it. The solution is a cross-referenced index system, manual or computerized. Again, the rewards are greatly in excess of the extra time required to install and use such a system. Most managers simply rely upon secretaries to compile files and recall them. This superior facility is another means of creating an edge.[10]

What to record

Any form of record is better than none at all. The best record, however, is one which facilitates accurate and comprehensive recall, months or even years later. Always note basics such as date, time and place, names of those present, names of those circulated, and so on. Such information can prove critical. For instance, a manager opposed to new departmental structures complained he had not been consulted about the proposal. Since discussions had commenced over a year previously, no one could remember for certain whether he had been consulted or not, but for the fact that his attendance had been recorded in all the notes of meetings. (One tiny point: always carry an A4 pad with you.)

It is a mistake to try to take *verbatim* notes of every meeting. Copious note-taking detracts from essentials. The art is to develop an ear for the key points. For example:

> Ambitions, oh, I'm not really ambitious. I mean I wouldn't mind if someone offered me a couple of non-executive directorships or a modest knighthood, you know something like that. But, ah well, that's all in the future, I mean I'm not really bothered what happens. It wouldn't bother me if I was still here in ten years' time. I've taken a couple of soundings here and there.

This is a highly significant conversation. Here is how to record it effectively:

> Note of conversation with ARS, 4/6/91.
> Location: his office. Present: self.
> Subject: ambition.
> ARS indicated:
> 1. seeking non-executive directorships
> 2. knighthood
> 3. is actively pursuing ie 'taking soundings.'
> NB. ARS feet shuffled when claiming to be unambitious

Not only does this form of note-taking clearly indicate what took place, economy with words makes it much easier to retrieve the information.

One of the benefits of economical note-taking is that it enables you to study the people you are dealing with, which may be more important than what they are saying. Here, the note-taker observed that the other party shuffled his feet when denying that he was ambitious. This is extremely significant behaviour, because it signals a mismatch between words and intention. People do give signals; these are important sources of intelligence to note and reflect upon. The only justification for lengthy scribble is that it buys time to think.

Power is enhanced if the other party is unaware that you have taken notes. It pays to train your memory to retain essential points, which is not as exacting as it sounds, as business discussions seldom concern more than six or seven issues. If this is impractical, a good compromise is to note details such as prices, delivery dates, and specifications. Then, when the other party is out of sight, write down some of the other things he mentioned.

Some old tricks

Information, like any other power resource, need not be real for it to be effective. What counts is:

not what you know, but what the other person believes you to know.

Pretending to possess a critical piece of information is an excellent means of disconcerting an opponent. This explains why the police question suspects separately. They can use isolation to pretend that one suspect has confessed, or that they know more than they actually do.

In management, one way of gaining an edge in an adversarial situation is to arm yourself ostentatiously with books, files, and at least two dozen clearly visible page-markers when you go to meet the other party. The other party, believing that you have done your homework, will suddenly feel rather less confident. Another trick is to fish for a piece of paper midway through a discussion and glance at it with a triumphant look. The effect is to immediately dent the opponent's confidence, as he believes that you may be about to produce evidence which will discredit him. What he does not know is that you are looking at a blank sheet.

Most of us have at some time been unable to read a report for a meeting, and consequently worry about being unable to answer questions. The solution to this problem is go grab a highlighter pen, randomly isolate a few paragraphs and scribble a few irritable looking notes in the margin. If you do this, and then open the document on the table, no one will dare ask you anything for fear of incurring a blistering response. The fact that you may have highlighted insignificant parts of the report or written 'Rubbish!' against perfectly sensible passages adds to strength because it makes others believe that your analysis is more penetrating than theirs!

Controlling information

The art of controlling information depends upon:

- knowing what to release;
- judging the best time to release it.

Everything depends upon circumstances; generally speaking, the best advice is to:

- promote favourable data;
- suppress unfavourable data.

If in doubt, keep things to yourself. For example, a junior work study officer learned through informal discussions with the trade unions that if a certain albeit incompetent manager was sacked, the unions would see it as the first move towards service closure. The work study officer decided against disclosing this information to the assistant director, as he disliked him. The manager was subsequently dismissed. A sharp deterioration in industrial relations followed, which caused the assistant director considerable anxiety and additional work.

If it becomes necessary to release unfavourable information, the following tactics may help:

1. Release it before someone else does

Limit the damage by taking charge. It is better that others hear the story from you than from someone else.

2. Preface bad news with good news

You might, for example, say, 'Before we start this meeting let me explain what we have done', and then detail two or three achievements. This immediately blunts criticism.

3. Do it gradually

Sudden shocks are dangerous: use your control over the information to release it bit by bit. That way, no one may even realize that a mistake has been made, far less the extent of it. For example, a finance officer once realized he had completely miscalculated the profit and loss account on a major contract. Rather than cause apoplexy and earn himself the sack, he quietly adjusted the accounts month by month until they reflected the true position.

bliss of ignorance

Although knowledge is power, ignorance can occasionally lead to success, because the ignorant are not restrained by fear of failure. For example, while it can be useful to know who else is on the shortlist for a job or is tendering for a contract, that knowledge is counter-productive if it undermines your confidence.

People blind to danger or ignorant of conventions sometimes succeed precisely because they venture into areas where others fear to tread. The turning point in the career of a most successful entrepreneur came when, as a nineteen-year-old serviceman, he walked into a hospital in Copenhagen carrying a new invention in the shape of a tubular bandage in a bag.[11] He believed he had a most useful product, but did not know who to contact. He therefore asked to see the top manager. The top manager duly appeared. Shortly afterwards, the serviceman found himself being whisked across the city in a chauffeur-driven car to discuss orders. Yet had he realized that senior hospital executives seldom agree to see nineteen-year-old servicemen, and without an appointment, he might not have asked.[12]

Summary

- Information is power.

- In power relations, both parties are usually dealing with incomplete information about one another. The aim is to achieve a margin of superiority.

- Information which you routinely have access to is a source of power.

- Where curiosity leads, follow.

- Few offices are properly secured. After-hours exploration can be rewarding.

- Much information is there for the taking. Power-seekers willingly expend the effort required to utilize it.

- Make sure your own office is secure — including the waste-paper bin.

- Listen rather than talk.

- Never reveal the pressure you are under.

- Sometimes more can be learned by not asking questions or appearing interested, especially where secretaries are concerned.

- Be alert to unusual activity or behaviour.

- Find out who talks to whom, and which people dislike one another.

- The most effective means of discovery is to get close to the person or situation.

- Power requires that information be:
  — recorded;
  — easy to recall;
  — easy to manipulate.

- The most important time to record information is at the start of a project or encounter.

- Power is further generated by recording first impressions, objectives, plans and worst fears.

- Always carry at least a notebook, pen and calculator.

- Cross-indexing is essential for recall and retrieval of information.

- Note-taking should focus upon the essentials.

- It is important to manage the release of bad news, ie:
  — take the initiative;
  — preface the announcement with good news;
  — release information gradually.

- Ignorance can be bliss.

INFORMATION QUESTIONNAIRE

Having read the chapter now re-test yourself:

1. **You are in negotiations with a company. Which of the following would interest you most?**

    a) the annual report
    b) an accountant's confidential report
    c) the merchant banker's correspondence file
    d) the chief executive's private diary.

2. **Your boss has a new secretary. Do you:**

    a) ask lots of questions
    b) ask how on earth he puts up with things
    c) say how much better organized the boss seems
    d) ask if he has any problems?

3. **You hear angry voices as you approach a door. Do you?**

    a) cough loudly
    b) pause and listen
    c) turn away
    d) walk straight in?

4. **A car you bought nine months ago is fast becoming a liability. Do you:**

    a) keep repairing it
    b) take it back to the garage and complain
    c) take it back to the garage and say you are getting bored with it
    d) explain to the garage that you are looking for something more expensive, as you have come into money?

5. **Which of the following do you carry?**

    a) personal organizer and pen
    b) pocket calculator
    c) hand-held dictating machine
    d) telephone recording attachment for hand-held machine.

6. **When transacting business or making enquiries, do you make notes of telephone conversations:**

    a) always

b) sometimes
c) rarely
d) never?

7. **An interesting job is advertised, with a telephone contact for enquiries. Do you:**

   a) wait and see if you are shortlisted
   b) pick up the phone at once
   c) use it as an opportunity to sell yourself
   d) jot down a few questions and then telephone?

8. **You are late for a meeting. Do you:**

   a) go straight there
   b) call at your office for the papers
   c) get your secretary to telephone and say you will be along in twenty minutes
   d) cancel?

9. **You are meeting a new contractor for the first time. Do you:**

   a) take detailed notes during the meeting
   b) concentrate on listening, but write down key points afterwards
   c) ask your secretary to take notes
   d) hide a tape recorder in the room?

10. **You discover that a plant which you had said was running at a serious loss is in fact returning a healthy profit. The mistake is due to inefficiencies within your own department. Do you:**

   a) rush out and spread the good news
   b) explain that new information has come to light which may show the position is not as bad as feared
   c) say nothing but modify the accounts gradually
   d) say nothing and let everyone continue to believe that the plant is losing money?

Answers overleaf.

Answers to Questionnaire

1. **d** — will tell you more than the rest put together.

2. **c** — concentrate upon building a relationship first.

3. **b**.

4. **c**. Do not reveal that you are desperate to get rid of the vehicle. Never d; if people smell money they will try and take from you.

5. If you are serious you have them all.

6. **a**.

7. **d**. The better prepared you are, the more you will learn.

8. **c** — you not only need the information but must also refresh your memory. D only damages your reputation.

9. **b**.

10. **c** — it may be good news, but it is also a hefty stick to beat you with. D will only make things worse.

Score before reading chapter ——

Score after reading chapter ——

References

1. Sterba, R L A (1978) 'Clandestine management in imperial Chinese bureaucracy,' *Academy of Management Review*, 3(1), pp. 69–78.
2. Neustadt, R E and May, E R (1986) *Thinking in Time: The Uses of History for Decision Makers*, Free Press, London.
3. Powis, D (1977) *The Signs of Crime: A Field Manual For Police*, McGraw-Hill, London.
4. Webb, E J, Campbell, T D, Schwartz, R D and Secherst, L (1966) *Unobtrusive Measures: Non-Reactive Research in the Social Sciences*, Rand McNally, Chicago. Contains a fascinating account of the types of clues people leave, and what can be deduced from them.
5. Kennedy, R (1965) *Thirteen Days: A Memoir of the Cuban Missile Crisis*, Norton, New York.
6. See Drummond, H (1991) *Effective Decision Making: A Practical Guide for Management*, Kogan Page, London, for further details of manipulation of information and emotion in decision making.
7. Neustadt and May, op. cit.

8. Lindblom, C E (1959) 'The science of muddling through', *Public Administration Review*, XIX(2), pp. 79–88.

9. Becker, H S (1960) 'Notes on the concept of commitment', *American Journal of Sociology*, 66, pp. 32–40.

10. Stibic, V (1980) *Documentation for Professionals: Means and Methods*, North Holland, Amsterdam. Contains useful ideas on how to establish an information retrieval system.

11. 'How innovation enabled Seton to put its finger on a healthy new market', *Financial Times*, (1982), November 12, p. 13.

12. Private conversation.

7
Expert power

Test your skills by answering the following questions:

1. **You need to buy some hardware to run a new computer software package. The company that is selling the software can supply the hardware. Do you:**

    a) ask for details and compare their prices and specifications with others'
    b) ask what they recommend
    c) ask them to quote for a package deal
    d) ask what discount they would give you?

2. **You are buying a house. The estate agent offers to recommend a solicitor and arrange a mortgage. Do you:**

    a) thank him for saving you the trouble
    b) tell him you will make your own arrangements
    c) indicate that you would be willing to consider quotations
    d) thank him and ask if he can arrange life assurance cover as well?

3. **You are buying some new machinery. A distributer telephones and says he can offer a 25 per cent reduction on a good brand name. He must, however, have an order today. Do you:**

    a) make sure he gets one
    b) ask him to fax a full set of specifications
    c) ask him what the big rush is
    d) tell him if he can make it a 30 per cent discount, he has an order?

4. **You are in dispute over patent rights. The other party tells you that they have taken counsel's opinion which indicates that they have an unassailable case. Do you:**

    a) suggest an out-of-court settlement
    b) ask on what basis the opinion rests
    c) take counsel's advice yourself
    d) say, 'See you in court'?

5. **You have commissioned a highly-respected surveyor to carry out a feasibility study on the potential of an old warehouse. Do you:**

    a) ask for an estimate of cost
    b) agree a precise brief and fee
    c) set a cost limit
    d) ask him to do what is necessary?

6. **You have commissioned a consultant to examine and make recommendations upon your information technology needs. The report, which took three months to produce, bears no resemblance to the brief and is useless. Do you:**

    a) refuse to pay
    b) demand a reduction
    c) tell the consultant to start again
    d) pay, and debit it to experience?

7. **You have received the surveyor's report on a property you hope to purchase. The report refers to a crack running down an outside wall and states, 'This could have been caused by subsidence. It is much more probable however that the movement occurred shortly after the property was built.' Do you:**

    a) abandon the purchase — it seems too risky
    b) ask the owner what he thinks
    c) talk to the surveyor
    d) go ahead?

8. **You wish to open an egg hatchery. Opposition is anticipated both from the 'greens' and from local businesses competing for the site. Who would you seek advice on planning permission from?**

    a) a local estate agent
    b) the local council office

    c)   a specialist London firm
    d)   work it out for yourself?

9. **You are in discussion with the artistic director of a theatre. He refuses to stage more than one popular play per season because, he says, to do more would undermine the artistic integrity of the theatre company. Do you:**

    a)   say you cannot see what difference it makes
    b)   tell him the issue is about viability
    c)   suggest that maybe he would like to assume responsibility for financial management
    d)   say, 'What more of that boring rubbish?'

10. **You have been asked to produce a business plan for your department. Do you:**

    a)   'look forward to the coming year'
    b)   'look forward to meeting the challenges of the coming year'
    c)   say: 'the coming year will be a critical period'
    d)   say: 'it is unlikely that we will still be in business next year'?

Expert power rests on trust. Trust in this context means:

> *the recipient believes the expert is serving the client's interests or ideals, and not his own.*[1]

This belief is extremely powerful. It blinds people from seeing that, when dealing with experts, they are in a power relation, and are vulnerable to manipulation. Patients, for example, typically assume that the doctor's prescription reflects the best possible treatment for their illness. It probably never occurs to them that they may be serving as guinea pigs for research, or that the doctor's prescribing habits are influenced by the drugs companies who fund lavish weekend 'seminars' abroad.

As in any power relation, in dealing with experts it is possible to do better or worse. Awareness of the dangers and techniques of exploitation helps redress the balance. Awareness begins with the recognition that expertise is potentially a smokescreen. The smokescreen serves:

> *to sell something.*

That something may be religion, moral guidance, a job, a car, an idea, a business, and so on. Whatever the issue is:

> *ask the expert for advice, and he will sell*
> *what he wants you to have.*

Some sellers do of course genuinely seek to serve their client's or customer's best interests. Such altruism, however, is by no means universal. Here is what a disenchanted employee of a high street retailer said when asked why he wanted to leave his present job:

> If a customer asks our advice on what video to buy, our instructions are to try and sell him an ——. It sickens me: although they're cheap, they're rubbish, always breaking down and customers then have to wait months for parts. Yet we have to pretend they're good because the mark-up is high.

Estate agents advertise that they are pleased to recommend a solicitor, or to organize mortgages and life assurance. Of course they are, given the commission they receive. Financial packages 'tailored to individual needs' are often those with the best 'rake-offs' and most dubious probity.[2]

Nor are professionals above exploitation. Vets, for instance, extol the benefits of animal health insurance because it provides *carte blanche* for elaborate treatment, regardless of its clinical value. It also facilitates a certain amount of rounding-up of bills. The vet, too, will be pleased to recommend a reliable insurance company — the one that pays him a commission.

Expert power is exploited in all walks of life. It is exalted when combined with some perceived moral duty on the part of the power-subject. Pregnant mothers, for example, are told, 'We want what's best for baby, don't we.' What this really means is we want what suits the medical staff, who play on the mother's perceived obligation to sacrifice her own comfort for what she believes will benefit the child.

Coping with expert power

Experts do not know everything

Having understood the existence of a power relation, the next step is to recognize that those professing expertise may be wrong. Expertise rests:

- not upon what someone knows; but
- upon what others believe he knows.

The first and most common reason whereby people are led astray is that in many situations:

no one knows.

Racing tipsters, for instance, inspire confidence through the naming of so-called 'dead certs'. Yet how *can* they know which horse will win the race? Property valuations, too, are guesswork, however confident the estate agent may sound. The outcome of law suits is often impossible to predict, however competent the lawyer. It is possible to obtain conflicting opinions from counsel, depending upon whether you are the plaintiff or the defendant. The value of a second-hand car varies dramatically, according to whether the customer's or the salesman's guide is used. Even the conclusions of the so-called hard sciences are based to some extent on guesswork. For example, many medical tests are far from 100 per cent reliable, though the results may be conveyed to patients as if they were.

How to become more knowledgeable than an expert

When taking advice or listening to recommendations, therefore, keep asking yourself:

how does he know?

The less there is to know, the more important it is to:

- conduct your own research and evaluation;
- make up your own mind.

Research is the most important means of empowerment. The best person to look after your interests is you. Time invested in studying the horses, comparing house prices, machinery specifications and so forth is time well spent. This is because it is the soundest means of making a good bargain, or at least avoiding an extremely bad one. Moreover, there is the satisfaction of subsequently being able to speak with equal or even greater authority on the subject than the seller.

Always aim to do just a little more research than seems necessary. The aim is to develop a feel for the issue, through talking to people, gathering data, and so forth. It is vital to anticipate your potential requirements and to become familiar with the pitfalls. In buying computer software, for example, it pays to think through what demands for information might be made. Likewise, in buying machinery, it is important to investigate the cost of spare parts. Some manufacturers, for instance, sell good machines quite cheaply. What they do not disclose, however, is that the cost of one replacement part may be as much as that of the original purchase.

Do not be put off by technical terms and jargon. You can master these the same as anyone else. The small print of most insurance policies, for instance, is easy to understand by those who take the trouble to read it. Reading alone, however, is not enough. You must consider what the words imply. For example, an accident policy which covers 'temporary total disablement', defined as 'disablement which wholly prevents the Insured Person from engaging in or giving attention to their usual occupation', does not cover a serious accident such as a car crash which immediately renders the insured person permanently unable to return to his occupation. This is because the disablement is not temporary. It is stressed that the time to discover such snags is *before* entering into a contract or other commitment.

Do not be daunted by the amount there is to learn. Formidable insight can be gleaned either by short intensive study, or the 'a little and often' approach. Just 20 minutes a day over, say, a month, will suffice to create a working knowledge of most issues.

Evaluation entails comparing alternatives. It is best to be systematic and to set out in table form prices, specifications, details of guarantees, and so on. This approach can be used for virtually any kind of decision, such as comparing job offers; assessing contractors' capabilities, and the purchase of anything from a fleet of lorries to a washing machine or an insurance policy. It sounds simple: it is simple, and in its simplicity rests the power, because highlighting similarities and differences in this way produces an analysis which is:

- objective;
- authoritative.

Analysis is only useful, however, if it informs decision making. Ignore unsubstantiated claims like 'These machines are the best on the market'; you know which machines offer best value for money. Information also provides a powerful basis for negotiation. Brokers, salesmen, employers, contractors and so on are often willing to reconsider when faced with unequivocal evidence that their offers are uncompetitive. Interestingly, however, analysis typically reveals that the most expensive products are not necessarily the best. This particularly applies to so-called, 'conspicuous consumption' items such as clothes, cars, pens, and other items of high snob value. So-called 'package deals' invariably repay scrutiny. Sellers exploit the commonly-held assumption that is it cheaper to buy in bulk or job lots. Those who take the trouble to investigate often find that this premise is ill-founded. The ultimate value of appraisal, however, is that whatever you decide to do in the end, there is the satisfaction of having chosen something because you wanted it, and not because someone sold it to you.

'Thirty-eight per cent'

As anyone who has marked exam scripts will know, wide variations exist in the skills and abilities of professionals. Twenty years ago, entry to dental school was quite possible with two grade E A levels, the minimum qualification for matriculation. Students admitted with those qualifications are now practising. Medical schools are reluctant to fail students because of the expense of training. Consequently, anyone scoring thirty-eight per cent passes, on the basis of being a border-line case. In fact, since examiners are loath to be destructive, thirty-eight per cent signals not a near pass, but an abysmal failure. A journalist researching barristers' performance was shocked by displays of stuttering and stammering, and advocates so unfamiliar with their briefs that they could not even recall their client's name in court, far less represent his case.[3]

Dealing with professionals

The point of all this is, never be overawed by professionals. Instead, be assertive, ie:

1. Do as much as possible yourself.

2. Ask questions.

3. Be prepared to obtain a second opinion.

4. Reserve time for reflection and pursuing enquiries.

5. Keep thinking 'thirty-eight per cent.'

Again, no one will look after your own interests better than yourself. People who airly declare, 'Oh I leave all that to the experts' almost invariably pay a price for neglecting their own affairs. One reason for this is that you know more about the issue than the expert. The vendor, for example, has seen the property he intends to buy; his solicitor has not. This means that the vendor is much better placed to spot, for instance, that the land registry details are inaccurate. A moment's reflection reveals that the solicitor cannot possibly know this.

Experts dislike being interrogated, because interrogation converts the relationship from one of authority to one of persuasion.[4] You cannot afford to be genteel. Asking questions and engaging in discussion helps assess the expert's intelligence, insight and interest in your problem. Besides, unless experts are challenged, they will do what suits them. Doctors may amputate because it is less trouble than performing an arterial bypass. Lawyers urge clients to plead guilty because it enables them to earn an easy fee, with no risk of exposing their own ineptitude.[5]

Experts do disagree with one another. Their judgement is sometimes motivated by pride, arrogance and spite. Moreover, as suggested earlier, some decisions inevitably involve a degree of guesswork. It is important to allow for this, and to seek a second opinion if you feel it would be useful or reassuring.

Never allow yourself to be pushed into making a decision. Hospital patients have been known to be bulldozed into submitting to surgery and other treatment without being given the opportunity to question its necessity, or to evaluate alternatives. There are few issues which cannot wait at least a day or two.

Most experts practise impression management. Indeed, the more shallow their knowledge, the more they may need to compensate. Ignore the plush surroundings, elegant suits and exaggerated mannerisms: keep thinking 'thirty-eight per cent'.

Fast deals make bad bargains

The worst decisions are invariably those made in a hurry. Sellers understand this, and use their knowledge to manipulate buyers. For example:

'Hurry hurry, offer ends today.'

The aim of manipulating time in this way is to prevent the buyer from considering alternatives. The technique is practised in all walks of life. The commonest examples in management are:

- 'I must have a decision by such-and-such a time.'
- 'If X is not done by such-and-such a time, there will be a complete disaster.'
- 'The absolute deadline is . . . .'

The best way of countering such arbitrary do-and-decide-by dates is to say:

If you want an answer in a hurry, the answer is 'no'.
However, if you give me time to think about it then maybe . . . .'

Never ask others to name a deadline. This only invites them to apply leverage. If a time-limit exists, they will tell you. For example, bargains are sometimes offered at the end of a financial year to inflate perform-ance. Even then, dates can be adjusted a little, so do not be rushed. Anyone unable to get beyond declamations such as 'We need a decision now', or 'We can't hold the offer' is bluffing. Likewise, ignore taunts such as 'We have another customer who is very interested'— there always is.

Never allow a salesman to 'speed things up' by writing tender speci-fications on your behalf. If you do, the salesman will use his superior knowledge to commit you to buying what he wants you to have. Then when it fails to meet your needs he will say, 'But that's what you ordered isn't it?' Incidentally, the true test of any bargain is:

> *how eager is the seller to take it back?*

The power of alternatives

Caveat emptor

One of the fundamentals of power relations is:

> *the seller invariably knows more than the buyer.*

Since the seller's knowledge is greater, so is his power. The sales con-sultant knows, for example, that his computer software demonstration package is only loaded with 50 items of data, so of course it appears fast and efficient. Once the contract is signed, it is left to the buyer to discover how it performs with a working load of 100,000 items. Likewise, the vendor of a house knows that the central heating system is broken, and that the springwater supply runs dry from April to September every year.

A margin of discretion

Doing your homework, as suggested earlier in this chapter, will do much to reduce such power differentials, but what of a situation where the seller says, 'Take it or leave it'? In many transactions, the doctrine of 'opportunity cost' eventually comes into play.[6, 7] A car dealer, for example, may hope to make a profit of £1,200 on a sale. He might be willing to accept £1,100, or even £1,000. However, as far as he is con-cerned, there is no point in accepting a lesser price, as he can probably sell the car to the next customer. This means it is important to be realistic in negotiating, by aiming to:

capitalize upon the margin of discretion.

Clearly it is a waste of time to haggle over the price of a tin of beans in a supermarket. The abundance of other customers is such that no justification exists for losing even one penny on a transaction — even at that level the opportunity cost is too high. Other dealings, however, present more room for manoeuvre. Realism begins with planning and intelligence-gathering, such as deciding how you will approach the other party, and listening for clues as to how important it is for him to sell. Generally speaking:

> *the more the other side needs to do a deal,*
> *the greater your power.*

The best means of obtaining concessions is:

> *bit by bit.*

Huge demands tend to provoke anger, which can result in a refusal to deal. Small ones, on the other hand, are more likely to be met, and can add up to a colossal amount. At the same time, be realistic about price. Note, however, that it can be counter-productive to use your power to drive an exceptionally hard bargain. Although the contractor may accept the job, he will take short-cuts on all the bits you cannot see.

Be prepared to walk away

Possession of alternatives is the best means of countering the seller's power and simultaneously protecting yourself from bad bargains.[8]

Develop alternatives long before negotiations commence.

Those who enter into bargaining knowing that they can afford to walk away have power. Developing alternatives simply means deciding:

- what you are prepared to pay;
- what you will do instead if the price is too high.

Possession of alternatives is a source of strength in all power relations. It is the means by which you retain ultimate control.[9]

All the king's horses and all the king's men

Experts live by earning a fee. Forget how prestigious the other party's solicitors or agents are:

> *if you have a case, you have a case.*

The corollary of this, of course, is if the other side is without a leg to stand on, no amount of expertise can change that. This may lead to attempts to intimidate the other party and lower his expectations. A common ploy is to suggest their case will be laughed out of court. The doubt sown, the next step is to offer a paltry sum in full and final settlement. A variation of this technique is where the buyer tries to obtain goods or services at a fraction of their value, by pretending they are of little worth.

Knowing your own strength is the only way to counter these unscrupulous ploys. However, you must not only know it, you must believe it steadfastly. Anyone who is told repeatedly, for instance, that they have no hope of winning, to say nothing of the bill for costs which they will be required to meet, is naturally bound to doubt themselves eventually. This is particularly true where the other party is wealthy, powerful, or a leading authority in the field. Train yourself to ignore such pressure. Let a hard look come into your eyes. If they are as unassailable as they say they are, why are they bothering to talk to you?

A splendid game of double-bluff

A theme of this book is that power need not be real for it to be effective. One risky but potentially highly-rewarding ploy based on this precept is to beat experts at their own game, by countering their bluff with a double-bluff. Imagine, for example, that you are in dispute over damages. You believe you have a 65 per cent chance of winning your claim for £200,000. The other side offers you £100,000 to settle out of court. Rather than haggle for, say, another £20,000 to £30,000, you could reject the offer contemptuously and say you will go to court unless the full claim is met. The risk is that the other party may let you do just that. More probably, however, they will believe that your case must be sound, as you are clearly prepared to sue to judgment, and so pay up.

Lord Wellington's celebrated response to a blackmailer 'Publish and be damned', is another example of the double-bluff technique. Again, there is a risk of the other party publishing. Since, however, the hold of blackmail rests upon fear of exposure, scornful dismissal of the threat may well dissolve that power.

Professional integrity

Although professionals are bound by strict codes of conduct, wheels nevertheless exist within wheels. People in the same line of business, in particular, tend to support one another. Upset one hospital consultant, for example, and you upset them all. For all you know, your banker may lunch with you one day, and with your deadliest business rival the next. Apply for a job in another department or organization, and regardless of what it says on the application form about confidentiality, the head of that department may well have telephoned your boss or someone else who knows you, to make a few enquiries.

It is vital to appreciate, therefore, that:

whoever they are, people put their own interests first.

Such behaviour is virtually impossible to prevent. The best advice is:

- to recognize where interests lie;
- to anticipate how they are likely to affect the other person's behaviour.

The most important thing to recognize is that people will seek to persuade or coerce you to sacrifice your interests in favour of theirs. An estate agent, for example, is not interested in seeing that he obtains the highest possible price for a client's property, despite what his glossy brochure proclaims. All he cares about is his commission. Having obtained the business, it makes little difference to him whether a house sells for £100,000 or £95,000. At, say, 1.25 per cent commission, instead of earning £1,250, he will get £1,187.50. He loses only £62.50, an insignificant sum which he will probably retrieve in any case by rounding up the advertising bill.

The vendor, however, is £5,000 poorer if he allows himself to be coerced by language such as, 'Surely, Mr Smith, that's an excellent deal we have procured for you; we don't get many offers like that you know.' Be firm in dealing with such pressure. If necessary be brutal and reply, 'It probably does seem a good offer to you. It enables you to sell this house and collect your commission with the minimum of effort.' Do not worry about offending him. Once your signature is on the contract, salesmen, estate agents and so forth immediately lose interest. Remember:

your money is good.

Confidentiality

Although in theory confidentiality is guaranteed when dealing with bankers, lawyers, stockbrokers and other professionals, it is unwise to depend upon it. Choose advisors who are at a distance. If, for example, you are seeking to acquire a lease upon a much sought-after office block in a small community, go and find a solicitor in the next town.

Blank cheques

Where money is involved, greed ultimately supervenes. Professionals and tradesmen alike will rip you off, given the chance. The only difference between them is that professionals fold the bill before they hand it to you. Exploitation results when the client places himself in the hands of the other party by giving him a blank cheque. Examples of blank cheques include:

1.   'Please do whatever is necessary' requests

Such requests are especially dangerous when circumstances are such that the client does not know what he is paying for. Instead, ask the expert for detailed recommendations with costs. Then go and do some research.

2.   Estimates instead of quotations

Always obtain quotations, never sanction work on the basis of an estimate. If you do, at best the invoice will reflect the top end of the estimate; more likely, it will exceed it by a substantial margin.

3.   Predetermined spending limits

Do not expect to see any change if you commission someone to act on this basis. They will spend the budget and then tell you more money is required to finish the job.

4.   Unpriced menus and unpublished tariffs

These are a sure sign of extortion, usually maintained by snobbery. Inquirers are dissuaded by haughty statements, such as 'People who eat here don't care about the price.'

5.   Ill-defined or non-existent specifications

Quotations alone are insufficient. The other party must specify in detail:

- what work will be carried out;
- when;
- by whom;
- to what standard.

This information can be hard to obtain, because professionals, contractors and tradesmen dislike being committed. Do not allow yourself to be put off. Even a simple task, such as fencing a field, holds the potential for short-cuts; dubious subcontracting, and so on. For instance, unless the whole job is rigorously specified, the contractor, and not the customer, decides, for example, whether timber or metal poles are used, the depth to which they are sunk; the quality of the wire, and so on.

Hide all traces of wealth and status when commissioning work, as these are guaranteed to add at least another 25 per cent to the bill.

Don't pay

If you are overcharged or swindled, sue only as a last resort. Much better to use your power to withhold payment. Nothing concentrates the other party's mind so effectively as an outstanding invoice. Do not yield to pressure. For example, a firm of consultants were briefed to make detailed recommendations as to the management and co-ordination of local council services in one of the poorest districts of the city. The resultant report, costing £150,000, was disgraceful. It consisted of a superficial description of familiar social problems and was totally devoid of any analysis or recommendations. The chief officer's management team were disgusted and said so. They listened aghast as the senior consultant then attacked them saying, 'I am sick of hearing such negative attitudes. This report is all you've got and you'd jolly well better realize that.' Fortunately the original brief had been carefully prepared, and so it was easy to prove the report's shortcomings.

Where the work is unsatisfactory but nevertheless usable, one option is to pay part of the bill and leave the other party to sue for the remainder. Usually they are never heard of again. The loss is accepted philosophically and added to the next customer's bill. (This approach works particularly well with small builders.)

Establishing effective relations with experts

Since experts are necessary it pays, despite all that has been said in this chapter, to establish effective working relations with them. The first and most essential point is to exert your power as client. This begins with:

playing hard to get.

Your custom will be more valued if the other party has to work to win it. Visit your prospective advisor before committing yourself, and explain that as the transaction is important to you, it is critical that you select an advisor in whom you have complete trust and confidence. I have a friend who interviews his prospective general practitioner before registering. Far from being resented, such assertiveness generally intrigues the other party. If the patient subsequently registers, the doctor is flattered. Above all, he has learned to respect the patient.

Expert advice is often expressed in reports or other written documentation. It is always a good idea to talk to the author, as he may tell you things informally which he cannot commit to writing. A surveyor, for example, might advise you off the record whether your proposed purchase is a bargain or a potential liability. Although, as mentioned earlier, experts dislike being interrogated, they generally enjoy talking about their work. They will respond well to enquiries if approached properly. Proceed as follows:

1. Begin by establishing a rapport with your advisor by thanking him for his work.

2. Check that he is free to speak with you for a few minutes.

3. Indicate that you are seeking one or two points of clarification.

4. Begin with a few simple factual questions.

5. As confidence builds, move the discussion on to what you really want to know.

Fight on your own midden

A common power ploy is the so-called 'exercise of professional judgement'. This works by using knowledge as a smokescreen for blocking or achieving change. Doctors, for example, practise it in order to get their own way by proclaiming, 'Patients will die unless . . .' (known in medical circles as 'shroud-waving').

The way to counter it is to:

redefine the issue.

If you allow yourself to be drawn into an argument over professional matters, you will lose. Change to a more favourable battleground by insisting that the issue is a managerial one.

Upon becoming an expert

So strong is expert-power that people will follow an expert's recommendations even when they believe the expert is wrong.[10] Becoming accredited as an expert therefore has advantages. The first rule is:

never make anything look easy.

When solicitors talk of 'scrutinizing the deed for defects in title', they imply that the task entails hours of concentrated, exacting work. It actually means checking that the prospective purchaser's name, property address and purchase price are correctly typed on to the form. Likewise, clients are led to believe that drawing up commercial contracts involves hours of intense labour, when most documents are standard forms.[11]

Such charades are necessary to preserve power and mystique. The technique basically rests upon skilful use of language, such as:

- 'a complete analysis is required'
- 'major reappraisal is required'
- 'this has major implications for . . .'
- 'this underpins our whole strategy'

You may know that 'complete analysis' or 'major reappraisal' means glancing through a few notes or doing some adds and take-aways. The other party does not, and will therefore accept what you say and be impressed.

Accreditation further involves:

the ability to speak with authority

Speaking with authority simply means sounding as if you are right. If you sound confident, others will have confidence in you, even if you are talking complete nonsense. The reason such a simple ploy succeeds is that it creates certainty. The philosopher Becker has argued that the ultimate source of power is man's fear of death. Becker contends that throughout history, men have surrendered their destiny to those who promise to engineer the world.[12] Shakespeare's character Macbeth, for instance, delivers himself to the witches in return for a promise to structure his fate, and guaranteed immortality.

Summary

- Expert power rests on the belief that the expert is pursuing the client's interests, and not his own.

- The exercise of expert power involves selling something, eg goods and services, religion, medical treatment, or a moral code.

- Ask a seller for advice and he will sell you whatever suits him.

- For many decisions, your own research and evaluation are as valid as any expert's.

- Expertise is often more apparent than real; remember, 'thirty-eight per cent'.

- Be assertive when dealing with professionals, ie:
  — ask questions;
  — get a second opinion;
  — refuse to be rushed.

- Never ask others to name deadlines, and if they do, ignore them.

- There is always another customer who is interested.

- Never allow a salesman to write contract specifications on your behalf.

- The true test of a bargain is, how eager is the seller to take it back?

- The seller always knows more than the buyer.

- If the seller has discretion over price, get it from him.

- The more the other side needs to do a deal, the greater your power.

- Demand concessions bit by bit.

- Possession of alternatives is the ultimate source of control.

- Never allow yourself to be bullied by another party's experts. If you have a case, you have a case.

- Playing poker is risky, but it can pay off handsomely.

- Although professionals are bound by strict codes of conduct, they have a living to earn. Know what their interests are and anticipate them.

- Never rely upon confidentiality.

- Never give anyone a blank cheque. Always obtain precise quotations for detailed briefs or specifications.

- If you are cheated, you have the power to withhold payment — use it, and let the other party do the running.

- Play hard to get when commissioning professionals.

- Never allow yourself to be drawn into an argument over professional matters. Fight on your own terrain.

- It pays to become accredited as an expert.

- Achieving accreditation requires:

  — the ability to make things look extremely difficult; and above all
  — to speak with authority.

CAN YOU DEAL WITH EXPERTS? QUESTIONNAIRE

Having read the chapter, now re-test yourself:

1. **You need to buy some hardware to run a new computer software package. The company that is selling the software can supply the hardware. Do you:**

   a) ask for details and compare their prices and specifications with others'
   b) ask what they recommend
   c) ask them to quote for a package deal
   d) ask what discount they would give you?

2. **You are buying a house. The estate agent offers to recommend a solicitor and arrange a mortgage. Do you:**

   a) thank him for saving you the trouble
   b) tell him you will make your own arrangements
   c) indicate that you would be willing to consider quotations
   d) thank him and ask if he can arrange life assurance cover as well?

3. **You are buying some new machinery. A distributer telephones and says he can offer a 25 per cent reduction on a good brand name. He must, however, have an order today. Do you:**

   a) make sure he gets one
   b) ask him to fax a full set of specifications
   c) ask him what the big rush is
   d) tell him if he can make it a 30 per cent discount, he has an order?

4. **You are in dispute over patent rights. The other party tells you that they have taken counsel's opinion which indicates that they have an unassailable case. Do you:**

   a) suggest an out-of-court settlement
   b) ask on what basis the opinion rests
   c) take counsel's advice yourself
   d) say, 'See you in court'?

5. **You have commissioned a highly-respected surveyor to carry out a feasibility study on the potential of an old warehouse. Do you:**

   a) ask for an estimate of cost
   b) agree a precise brief and fee
   c) set a cost limit
   d) ask him to do what is necessary?

6. **You have commissioned a consultant to examine and make recommendations upon your information technology needs. The report, which took three months to produce, bears no resemblance to the brief and is useless. Do you:**

   a) refuse to pay
   b) demand a reduction
   c) tell the consultant to start again
   d) pay and debit it to experience?

7. **You have received the surveyor's report on a property you hope to purchase. The report refers to a crack running down an outside wall and states, 'This could have been caused by subsidence. It is much more probable however that the movement occurred shortly after the property was built.' Do you:**

   a) abandon the purchase — it seems too risky
   b) ask the owner what he thinks
   c) talk to the surveyor
   d) go ahead?

8. **You wish to open an egg hatchery. Opposition is anticipated both from the 'greens' and from local businesses competing for the site. Who would you seek advice on planning permission from?**

   a) a local estate agent
   b) the local council office
   c) a specialist London firm
   d) work it out for yourself?

9. **You are in discussion with the artistic director of a theatre. He refuses to stage more than one popular play per season because, he says, to do more would undermine the artistic integrity of the theatre company. Do you:**

   a) say you cannot see what difference it makes
   b) tell him the issue is about viability
   c) suggest that maybe he would like to assume responsibility for financial management
   d) say, 'What more of that boring rubbish?'

10. **You have been asked to produce a business plan for your department. Do you:**

    a) 'look forward to the coming year'
    b) 'look forward to meeting the challenges of the coming year'
    c) say: 'the coming year will be a critical period'
    d) say: 'it is unlikely that we will still be in business next year'?

Answers opposite.

References

1. Wrong, D H (1979) *Power: Its Forms Bases and Uses*, Basil Blackwell, Oxford.
2. Clarke, M 'The regulation of estate agency'. Paper presented at the Liverpool Conference on Fraud, Corruption and Business Crime, April, 1991.
3. Zander, M (1989) *A Matter of Justice: The Legal System in Ferment*, Oxford University Press, Oxford.
4. Wrong, op. cit.
5. Hazell, R (1978) *The Bar on Trial*, Quartet Books, London.
6. Pruit, D G (1981) *Negotiation Behavior*, Academic Press, New York.
7. Rafia, H (1982) *The Art and Science of Negotiation*, Harvard University Press, Cambridge, Mass.
8. Fisher, R and Ury, W (1983) *Getting to Yes*, Hutchinson, London.
9. Bacharach, P and Baratz, M S (1970) *Power and Poverty: Theory and Practice*, Oxford University Press, New York.
10. Schwenck, C R (1988) 'Effects of devil's advocacy on escalating commitment', *Human Relations*, 41 (10), pp. 769–82.
11. Joseph, M (1955) *The Conveyancing Fraud*, Michael Joseph, London.
12. Becker, E (1975) *Escape from Evil*, Collier Macmillan, London.

Answers to questionnaire

1. **a** — do anything else and you will only get what they want to sell you. You can still negotiate later, and from a position of power through having done your homework.

2. **b** — maintain your independence.

3. **b** — find out exactly what you are being offered first.

4. **d** will take the wind out of their sales.

5. **b** — anything else and you will pay dearly, no matter how prestigious the firm.

6. **a.**

7. **c** — you need to know what 'much more probable' means.

8. **c** — opt for a or b, and the news will be all over town.

9. **b** — do not get dragged into an argument on his terms. Say d and he will never speak to you again.

10. **c** makes it sound difficult without being negative. Never say d, even if it is true, as they will sack you and find someone who will tell them what they want to hear.

Score before reading chapter: ——

Score after reading chapter: ——

8

The power of diplomacy

DIPLOMACY QUESTIONNAIRE

Do you qualify for CD plates? Find out by answering the following questions?

1. **A colleague has just circulated a report which is a dreadful mess. He meets you on the corridor and asks what you think of it. What do you say?**

   a) 'Fine, excellent, just what we need.'
   b) 'It's awful.'
   c) 'Excellent, I have one or two tiny suggestions which you might be interested in.'
   d) 'I have not had time to read it yet.'

2. **You have forced an incompetent employee to resign. At the farewell dinner do you:**

   a) make a speech praising his work and regretting that his health prevented him from finishing it
   b) make a pleasant speech but without any reference to the employee's work
   c) omit the speeches
   d) develop a diplomatic illness and get someone else to make the presentation?

3. **A colleague is trying to form a breakaway department. He asks what your position would be if he were successful. What do you say?**

   a) you would definitely be interested in joining, and write a paper showing how your respective functions could be merged

b) wish him well and say you would be interested in further discussion when the time comes

c) you are happy as you are

d) tell him he cannot succeed.

4. **You turned down a job offer a year ago because of a residency requirement, and have since regretted the decision. You then receive a telephone call asking if you are still interested in the job, which has unexpectedly become vacant again. What do you say?**

   a) 'Yes, I will accept on the terms previously offered.'
   b) 'I will accept only if the residency requirement is waived.'
   c) 'What are you prepared to offer?'
   d) 'I am willing to discuss it.'

5. **You are the owner of a dog kennel. One of your clients asks which is your favourite breed. Do you:**

   a) say 'I love all dogs' and then change the subject
   b) name your favourite breed
   c) name the client's favourite breed
   d) say 'I hate all dogs'.

6. **A less well qualified and experienced rival has beaten you to promotion. Do you:**

   a) lodge a grievance
   b) publicly doubt the other person's qualifications and capability
   c) send him a note of congratulations
   d) ask him for a job?

7. **A friend invites you to admire his new sports car. You have never seen anything so ugly. Do you say:**

   a) 'You paid how much for it?'
   b) 'It's a fine example of its kind.'
   c) 'I'm jealous.'
   d) 'I don't suppose you'd want to sell it to me?'

8. **You are looking for another job because you are tired of trying to operate with inadequate resources. What would you say to prospective employers?**

   a) be honest about your reason for wanting to leave
   b) say nothing unless asked, in which case, be honest about it
   c) explain that one of the things you like about your present job is the challenge of managing with minimal resources
   d) try and prevent your prospective employer from getting a word in edgeways.

9. **A new employee has just submitted a set of costings. They are nothing like what you wanted. Do you say:**

   a) 'This is quite good, it just needs tidying.'
   b) 'Obviously I did not make myself clear when I asked you to do this job.'
   c) 'This is complete rubbish.'
   d) 'You're sacked.'?

10. **You are convinced that one of your branch offices is over-staffed, but feel unable to exercise control from a distance. Would you:**

   a) involve the branch staff more in your own management meetings
   b) transfer some of the staff to headquarters where you can supervise them
   c) start holding management meetings at the branch
   d) send in a work-study team?

An army platoon became hopelessly lost out in open country, thanks to an inexperienced officer. The situation was growing dangerous as nightfall was approaching and the company were many miles from base and without shelter. Pride prevented the officer from admitting his incompetence. Army discipline prevented his troops from taking control. Their mutual plight was finally resolved when the sergeant said to the officer, 'May I see your compass sir. I think there may be something wrong with it.'

Generally speaking, a diplomat is generally speaking. Diplomacy, however, involves more than being tactful, though tact is certainly an important attribute of a diplomat. Diplomacy is about:

- recognizing situations for what they really are;
- recognizing people for what they really want.

Recognizing reality

Perceiving reality is the key to skilful navigation of the waters of life. It requires the ability to distance oneself in order to see things not as you might wish to see them, or as others would have you see them, but for what they actually are. The critical question is:

what business are you in?

Medical students, for example, have to recognize that success is not about healing people, but turns upon passing exams.[1] Learner drivers are not in the business of being taught to drive *per se*, but in how to pass a test requiring them to operate a vehicle at 29 mph and do everything correctly. Likewise, police forces often find themselves in the business of producing satisfactory statistics, rather than actually preventing and detecting crime.

Playing the game

Recognizing reality and the pressures that other people are under means seeing matters as a game, and playing accordingly. The key to success is:

to do what is wanted.

Whatever a local councillor might say about serving the community, for example, his prime concern is to be re-elected, and possibly to become, or to remain, powerful within the council. The last thing a councillor wants to know, for instance, is that the swimming pool in his ward is costing a fortune to maintain. What he wants are facts and figures to justify the pool's existence. An adroit administrator will see that he gets them.

The same applies in management. It is essential to discover what the game is, and to play it. If the priority is expansion, reports on potential cost savings are unlikely to be valued. On the other hand, if survival is all, talk of expansion will only irritate powerful others.

Being seen to play the game

Playing the game alone is insufficient. What counts is to be seen to play it. Credit accrues:

- not for what you do, or try to do;
- only for what you are seen to have done.

Credit is seldom awarded to those who hide their light under a bushel. Although hard work and achievement may speak for themselves, it pays to force others to notice you.

Further:

> *evidence of achievement and actual achievement are not necessarily synonymous.*

An army officer, for example, insisted that desks be cleared every Friday afternoon. An astute corporal realized that all the officer wanted to see was a desk without any paper on it. So, instead of spending half an hour tidying papers away, he merely stuffed them into a large envelope and posted it to himself. At inspection the officer would say, 'That's what I like to see, a tidy desk.'

Likewise, a manager's task might be to negotiate a new bonus scheme. Provided he can show that negotiations have taken place, and that an apparently sensible scheme has been agreed, little else matters. Evidence of achievement has been created. No one will worry about whether the new scheme is wise in the long term, or the machinations that led up to the agreement, or whether it took an afternoon or six weeks to complete.

Many people render themselves ineffective by striving to do everything the hard way. The reason is probably cultural; the western work ethic leads people to feel distrustful about strokes of luck.[2] Yet if all a client or a superior wants is, for instance, a box of apples, why spend all day picking them from the trees when it is much quicker and easier to gather up a few windfalls?

Playing the game means supplying:

> *what the other person wants to see or hear.*

When someone wants to see increased profits, they want to see profits increased. They become impatient with people who tell them what the problems are. Conversely, they warm to those who provide quick and easy solutions.

Providing solutions means listening and probing very delicately in order to ascertain what the other person is really looking for. The word 'really' is important, as the other party's true purpose may be veiled. If someone wants to see increased profits, for example, do they mean they want the organization to become more efficient, or do they merely want to see 5 per cent, say, become 10 per cent? The distinction is vital: the worst thing that an inexperienced enthusiast can do is to upset the whole workplace by carrying out a major review, when a swift adjustment to the method of calculating depreciation can achieve the objective.

Some readers may regard this as dishonest. The problem is, if you are unwilling to comply, you may be regarded as inept and unhelpful.

Moreover, someone else will only supply what is wanted and get the credit. The real rogues are the people inviting the deception. They get the information they deserve.

'Wilt no one rid me?'

A counsellor once said to a client, 'Now that you have told me your problem, let me reflect it back.' The client replied, 'I don't want it reflecting back. I want rid of it.' The moral of this story is that people are often looking for:

something to get them off the hook.

Trade union officials, for instance, must keep their members content without dissipating their energies and discrediting themselves in pursuit of hopeless cases. Power-seekers recognize that the other person's problem is their problem. For example:

> After long discussion and several adjournments, the Management said they appreciated the Trade Union Side's vigorous representation of their members' case. They felt though that it would be wrong, in principle, to make an exception.

This minute serves as more than a record of decisions. The real intention is to provide the 'Trade Union Side' with something they can use to prove to their members that they have made strenuous efforts to prosecute their case. In other words, it gets the trade unions off the hook.

Here is another example:

> I refer to our telephone conversation on Tuesday concerning Mr Smith's grading claim. This issue has been well aired in two grievance hearings which unequivocally rejected Mr Smith's case. The procedure has now been exhausted and therefore the issue is closed.

This communication looks like a curt rebuke to Mr Smith's shop steward. Mr Smith, however, might have been surprised by the conversation which led up to it:

Shop Steward: I've got Jim Smith on at me again about his bloody grade. Is there anything you can do?

Manager: Tell you what, I'll write to you saying 'sod off'. You can show him the letter and then you might get peace.

Shop Steward: Good idea.

Manager: I'll draft it out and read it to you over the phone before I send it. How's that?

Shop Steward: Great. Anything to get him off my back.

See it as they see it

People are not always as honest as this shop steward about the pressures they face. One way of finding out is to:

imagine yourself in the other person's position.

The idea is to literally think your way into the other person's mind, in a similar way to actors who try and become the charaters they play. This is a very powerful technique, because it enables power-seekers to:

1. Obtain a realistic perspective.

2. Modify their behaviour accordingly.

3. Predict how the other party will respond.

4. Envisage alternative scenarios.

5. Foresee outcomes.

Of these, the first is the most important, because everything else flows from it. Deep involvement in issues or even the hurly-burly of everyday life distorts perception. It is all too easy to see what we want to see, and believe what we want to believe, regardless of what objective conditions indicate. The lover, for example, persuades himself that his partner will be pleased to see him, despite the fact that he abruptly terminated their relationship two years ago and has not been in contact since. Likewise, an employee may imagine that his manager attaches the same importance to processing his salary claim as he does.

Misguided perceptions lead to inappropriate actions and unjustified expectations, which in turn result in failure or even disaster. The lover, unprepared for a cold reception, walks angrily away, thus destroying any possibility of a reconciliation. The employee, having submitted his claim, assumes his manager will deal with it with all despatch, and so does nothing for a year. He then finds to his dismay that the claim is still in his manager's in-tray.

Power-seekers try and avoid such mistakes by thinking about what they are trying to achieve and how it affects others. A negotiator, for example, may perceive that the trade unions distrust him. He therefore recognizes that it will take time to build relations and so postpones discussion of important proposals until the time seems right. Meanwhile, he uses his time to obtain agreements on minor topics, building confidence and thus paving the way for future success.

Two quick and easy means of predicting outcomes are to ask:

1. What's in it for the other person?

2. Do inputs match required outputs?

It was stressed in chapter five that rewards are powerful motivators. The reverse is true, ie it is unrealistic to expect efforts and commitment from another person unless a suitable pay-off exists.

Elementary mathematics teaches that it is impossible to take something from nothing and get something. Yet it is all too easy to delude oneself into expecting results when the requisite investments are missing. Shakespeare foresaw the inevitable result of such self-deception:

King Lear: This is nothing fool.
Fool: Then 'tis like the breath of an unfee'd lawyer — you gave me nothing for it.

Public utterings and private mutterings

Attitude is a priceless asset. The most powerful attitude is:

a positive one.[3]

This means presenting and responding to issues in an optimistic and confident manner. A positive attitude means finding something good to say about everything and everyone. Here, for example, is what one employee felt about his job:

I can't stand it any longer. My boss doesn't listen. He doesn't care about people, he doesn't know how to relate to them or how to get the best out of them. He seems to think we have an army of staff to do what he wants, which wouldn't be so bad, but he changes his mind every five minutes. I have been on tranquillizers for the last six months.

His resignation letter, however, read:

I would like to take this opportunity to thank you for all the support you have given me over the past two years. I have enjoyed working with you and have learnt a great deal from you.

The same applies when attending job interviews. Always present a positive reason for seeking to join a new employer, and always be positive about your existing job, even if you hate it. For example.

1. Yes it is true that I have been made redundant and that is why I am looking for a job. However, my work is important to me, and therefore I have no intention of accepting any old job. What attracts me about this one is . . .

2. I enjoy my existing job and I am in no hurry to leave it. At the same time, I feel I have given my best to it and learned as much as I am going to learn, and therefore it is time to move on.

3. I saw my existing job as a short-term move. I was aware when I accepted the appointment that it was far from ideal in many ways. However, the experience it offered far outweighed the disadvantages and I am extremely glad I took the opportunity. However, having given my best to it and obtained the experience, I am ready to move on.

Even in casual conversation, always give the impression that things are going well. Never reveal anything that might be interpreted as desperation, be it to leave, to obtain a contract, find new business, etc. Such guardedness does result in loneliness. This is a price power-seekers are willing to pay. Equally, however, avoid going to the other extreme of appearing too confident or successful, as this only stimulates jealousy.

Always conduct yourself impeccably in public. If someone beats you to a job, for instance, always make a show of congratulating them, however angry or disappointed you feel. Never reveal negative feelings. This only puts others on their guard, or enables them to exploit you by playing on your emotions.

Keeping your options open

A colleague solicits your approval for his proposed departmental restructuring which, coincidentally, he would head up. It seems a good idea, especially as he mentioned something about there being something in it for you. That same afternoon, however, another colleague shows you his plan for a restructure, one which implies him as head of department. He too asks for your support and says something about needing a reliable deputy. Faced with such conflicting pulls upon loyalty, what should a power-seeker do?

Organizations are riddled with ambiguity and uncertainty. No one can predict how matters will turn out. Many people cannot cope with so many unknowns. They seek stability by pledging themselves to whoever promises certainty. Faced with a scenario such as the one just described, they rush to pledge themselves one way or another. Power-seekers, however, enjoy suspense and seek to profit from it. They are able to distance themselves, and recognize that people will seek to canvass support for all sorts of projects and causes. Power-seekers further recognize that in doing so, others have but one objective, ie:

to further their own ends.

Armed with this basic assumption about human nature, power-seekers survive and prosper by:

keeping their options open

We now examine what this means.

Look one way and row another

Retaining options involves recognizing the reality of change, and its implications. Sentimentality and loyalty are expensive luxuries when ice-caps begin to melt. As the old king's health wavers, for example, the barons remain loyal, while simultaneously giving their attention to the succession.

Keeping your options open means budgeting for all probable scenarios, however unpalatable these may be. For instance, if the company that you work for is failing, then redundancy is a possibility. It may be unlooked for but it has to be faced. Those who make contingency plans have the highest chance of survival, and even of benefiting from catastrophe. Ignore predictions like, 'It will never happen.' The people who become victims of events are those who bury their heads in this way.

Budgeting for alternative scenarios entails identifying alternative outcomes. People typically become riveted by either/or possibilities. When two athletes or horses are battling to win, few notice the third competitor stealing up from behind. Power-seekers remain alert to such possibilities. The place to look for surprises is invariably in some odd corner of the organization. It is predicted, for example, that the Third World War will not be triggered by a confrontation by the so-called 'superpowers', but by an upset in a remote part of the globe.[4]

How to say 'Yes' to everyone without committing yourself

Keeping options open enables power-seekers to keep everyone else dangling, while feathering their own nests. The most useful word for this purpose is 'maybe' closely followed by 'soon' and 'when the time is right'. Expressing interest encourages others to reveal their plans, without binding you.

Never commit yourself until there is absolutely no alternative, even when you are clear as to the right decision. Everything changes in time. Today's ludicrous job offer is potentially tomorrow's golden opportunity. Likewise, today's golden opportunity is potentially tomorrow's crown of thorns. Always leave yourself room to manoeuvre, and remember:

> There are old diplomats,
> And there are bold diplomats,
> But there are no old bold diplomats.
>   (Clarke, E (1973) *Corps Diplomatique*, Allen Lane, London)

How to extricate yourself

Here are some possibilities, should it be necessary to extricate yourself:

Ten ways to get yourself off the hook

1. 'What was right (or would not have been right) two years ago is very different from what is appropriate today.'

2. 'When those changes were made, never at any time did I say the process was complete.'

3. 'I have reconsidered my decision in the light of . . .'

4. 'Had this been known at the time . . .'

5. 'This could not have been predicted when the original decision was made.'

6. 'What I said/meant was . . .'

7. 'There was never any commitment to . . .'

8. 'The original decision had to be taken quickly. Much more quickly than I would have liked.'

9. 'It was always recognized that this would be a temporary move.'

10. 'Since then, new opportunities have arisen and it would be foolish to ignore them, even if it means revising earlier policies.'

Balancing opposing factions

Those who have to deal with opposing factions are vulnerable to being killed in the cross-fire, though they are also presented with opportunities. A former senior colleague of mine kept a pencil sharpened at both ends. This he explained symbolized the Janus face of the personnel office. 'As far as the trade unions are concerned, we support them. As far as management are concerned, we support them. In fact,' he explained, 'what we are really doing is getting what we want.'

The key to power in this context is:

divide and rule.

This entails acting as broker for both parties. Power brokers succeed by:

*secretly agreeing with everybody, and simultaneously,
boxing them into a corner.*

Imagine, for example, being caught in an argument between your boss and another colleague over whether to stock goods of poor quality but high mark-up. To your colleague you say:

'*You are absolutely right, we must maintain standards.*'

And to the boss:

'*You are absolutely right, we must be pragmatic.*'

Then at the meeting you say:

'*I think you both have a point.*'

This works because each side is unaware that the other has tried to solicit your support. Moreover, neither person can take exception, because you agree with them. Having thus boxed them into a corner, the next step is to propose a third option, ie your own preferred solution.

Another application of divide-and-rule is to manipulate powerful factions into destroying one another. Imagine a small gunboat facing two large enemy ships in the dark. Each large ship is unaware of the other's presence. If the gunboat tries to attack either it will be destroyed. On the other hand, if it runs between the two large vessels firing its guns in the air each ship might think that the enemy is attacking it, and fire back. That way, the big ships might sink one another.

Applying this principle to people is easy. A mere whisper to A, for example, that B is secretly trying to undermine him, and vice versa, may suffice. Likewise, an indication to a trade union that a rival union is seeking to do a secret deal with management, and vice versa, is enough to achieve the objective of divide-and-rule.

Diplomatic behaviour

Tact means making others feel comfortable with you. Such consideration leads to power, because people tend to trust and reward those with whom they feel comfortable. A key skill is:

compensating for other's deficiencies.

King John, for example, was a small man. Court diplomats therefore wore slippers and stood stoop-shouldered in his presence. King Edward VII, upon seeing a foreign guest throwing spinach tips upon the floor, immediately followed suit. Colleagues of an employee who suffered from breathlessness discreetly waited until he had been in the room a few minutes before speaking to him.

Diplomats are also adroit at making themselves agreeable without compromising their integrity or their authority. This revolves around:

- conveying criticims in a way that the other person can accept;
- saying what people want to hear without being untruthful.

On the first point, silence is invariably the best means of preserving relations. Failing that, restraint is essential. Imagine, for example, dealing with a customer who is trading in a car which has suffered one or two minor collisions. The most diplomatic approach is to pretend not to have seen the dents and scrapes. However, if it is necessary to lower expectations, a simple 'Oh dear, been in the wars' will suffice. Describing the vehicle as a 'battle-wagon' is not recommended.

Another way of conveying criticism in a diplomatic manner is to point out the error and then take the blame. For example:

- 'Obviously the brief I gave you was ambiguous.'
- 'Maybe I did not make myself clear.'
- 'I am sorry if I have confused you.'
- 'Perhaps I should have explained it better.'

If a report or other submission is partial, it may be appropriate to say, 'It's fine as far as it goes.' If it is nonsense or misses the point, say that you do not understand it. If faced with a hopeless case, try and avoid becoming involved. Let someone else do the unpleasant work. If it is essential to be overtly negative, use the following formula:

1. Begin by mentioning one or two good things.

2. Then deal with the bad things.

3. Round off with one more good thing.

For example

1. Two good things

   The work you have done in implementing the restructure has been excellent. I was especially pleased with the way in which you took such an effective lead in making sure that the timetable was observed.

2. Two bad things

   What you need to learn is that it is easy to make a mistake when you are under pressure, by not checking the procedure and not checking things out with me. You need to make sure you do both of those things if the issue is complex or unusual.

3. One more good thing

   Having said that, I'm delighted by the way in which the whole exercise has gone. It couldn't have been accomplished as fast and as well without you.

Do not be drawn into unproductive argument. Hear the person out, then say, 'I have nothing to add to that.' Then move on to another point.

Nothing but the truth, but not the whole truth

Saying what people want to hear without being untruthful is a valuable skill. The trick is to:

- find something positive;
- comment upon it.

A parishioner, for example, once invited the vicar to admire his garden. The vicar thought the garden looked horribly regimented. Since he could neither offend his host nor be untruthful, he said, 'It's very formal.' His host was delighted, as formality was the very thing he had tried to create. Similarly, a professional once showed his colleague a mammoth-sized report he was proud of. The latter privately thought the whole thing amounted to overkill. However, he replied, 'I see what you mean about leaving no stone unturned. Looks like a lot of work went into that.' This response gave pleasure, as the writer prided himself upon his thoroughness.

Anticipating how others may perceive your behaviour

In times of national and international crisis, all eyes and ears are trained upon statesmen as people try and deduce their attitudes and intentions from their words and behaviour.

The same happens in daily life. People watch constantly for signals. Power-seekers must therefore consider how their:

gestures, words and decisions may *be interpreted.*

It is all too easy to reveal oneself in an unguarded moment. Princess Margaret's scandalous involvement with Peter Townsend was deduced by onlookers when she brushed dandruff from his shoulders during the coronation.[5] An employee who delayed completion of his performance appraisal form because 'everything is changing' unwittingly betrayed that he was looking for another job.

It is important to guard against giving others the wrong impression. Ask about holidays or flexi-time at a job interview, for instance, and you may be judged as lazy. State the obvious on a particular issue and others may conclude that your knowledge is shallow.

No infallible means exists of avoiding such mishaps, not least because people are sometimes unconscious of their behaviour. You may not be aware, for example, of raising your hands to you face every time certain individuals speak in a meeting. Others will have noticed, however, and will have drawn the correct conclusions. The best advice is to think before you speak or act. Note, however, that should you commit any indiscretion, retraction may make matters worse. Remember the saying:

if you put your foot in it, leave it there.

It is also important to avoid laying yourself open to criticism. Spend too much time out of the organization, for example, and you may be seen as an absentee landlord. Spend too much time in the office, however, and you may be castigated as a belt-and-braces bureaucrat. Leave subordinates to get on with their work and they will say you take no interest in things. Try and support them, on the other hand, and you will be seen as overbearing and afraid to delegate. Use your initiative and you become branded as wayward and uncontrollable. Wait for instructions and others will say you lack gumption.

The best way to resolve these double-bind situations is through discussion and agreement with others.[6] Failing that, try and steer a middle course.

The diplomatic subordinate

The dead apprentice

The village church of Rosslyn in Scotland contains a beautifully carved pillar. The story is that when the pillar was commissioned, the master carver was so overawed by the task that he journeyed to Italy to study the architecture and find a design. While the master was away, his apprentice saw the finished pillar in a dream and set to work. When the master returned, he found the carving complete. The pillar was beautiful, beyond anything the master could have produced. He expressed his gratitude by murdering the apprentice.

The moral of this story is:

> *if you are as good as, or better than your boss, you must use your talents very carefully.*

This applies to everything, including skill, intelligence, car, clothes, connections, and achievements. It is surprising what petty jealousies influence people. A colleague of mine, for instance, once confessed to secret anger when his deputy appeared on the day of a royal visit wearing a better suit than his own. The deputy was promptly despatched across town on an errand.

Your 'umble servant

Disgruntled lecturer to college Principal:
'Most of us feel that if we could find a better hole, we'd go to it.'

Vice-Principle to lecturer in a private conversation afterwards:
'If you'd said any more you would have dug one for yourself.'

It is possible to win an argument with the boss, but at the expense of losing the war. Despite what they may say about participation, few managers really appreciate being challenged. If challenge is unavoidable, preface it with 'As you know . . .' Avoid strident expressions like 'Why don't you . . .' as these are seldom persuasive. Instead, emphasize the other person's power by saying, 'Have you considered . . .', or better still, 'Would you consider . . .'.

The best way to get someone to accept your idea is to make them feel it is their own. For example, 'Have you ruled out the option you mentioned earlier of . . .'. It is immaterial if this is the first time the other person has heard the suggestion. Most people have a healthy capacity for self-deception. Elevation, too, is flattering, because people like to see themselves as actors on a grand stage. The idea of 'ruling out' and possessing 'options' (a more powerful word than 'idea') makes them feel important and in control, even if the issue only concerns the refreshment arrangements for an evening meeting.

How Claudius survived

Emperor Claudius survived the knives and hemlock which claimed the lives of so many of his contemporaries by using his stammer to make himself appear a harmless idiot. Since no one was afraid of him, no one thought to conspire against him.

This story explains why organizational lightweights are often successful. Jealousy stems from fear. Fear stems from feelings of personal inadequacy. People react negatively to those whom they fear, and positively towards those with whom they feel comfortable. Lightweights succeed because they make others feel competent and strong. Never under-estimate these individuals, however. Some may not be over-burdened with brains, but many are clever enough to hide their intelligence. Lightweights tend to be malleable characters, which enables them to survive as they can bend with every change of the prevailing wind, swaying but never breaking through storm and tempest. The proud and self-righteous, on the other hand, are incapable of flexibility. Like an overly-rigid tower, they are prone to collapse when strained.

Sharing the power and the glory

As Lady Bracknell observes in *The Importance of Being Earnest*, 'The only people who complain about society are those who can't get into it.' The same applies to success. Success creates resentment, especially when others feel excluded and therefore alienated. Alienation stimulates destructiveness. Power-seekers are therefore advised to try and minimize potential harm, by sharing their achievements.

Sharing, even if only in a small degree, dilutes animosity. This is because it creates involvement, by converting bystanders into stakeholders. This explains, for example, why governments encourage home-ownership. The aim is to give as many people as possible a share in society and a reason to identify with rights of ownership and all that these entail. Similarly, many companies operate employee share purchase schemes to try and give everyone a stake in the business.

Applying this precept to the individual level, if you win an award, for example, accept it not for yourself, but on behalf of the organization. Furthermore, include the whole office or team in the photograph. Likewise, when accepting congratulations, emphasize, and be seen to emphasize, the contribution of your management team or staff. If you pass an exam, share the pleasure by buying buns for the coffee-break.

As you become more powerful, make staff feel that they too are in the ascendant. Let them identify with your success and share some of its fruits. Emphasize their standing within the organization, for example, and ensure they are better informed than their compeers in other departments. If you buy a new desk, circulate the furniture catalogue so that everyone has the opportunity to profit. Make others see that they have a vested interest in your continuing prosperity.

Note, however, that there are limits to what a power-sharing strategy can achieve. Never:

- flaunt success;
- upstage more powerful others.

A chief executive of a Labour-controlled council, for instance, might look incongruous driving a battered Datsun. However, he is more likely to survive than one who makes his £80,000-a-year salary obvious. Pride, remember, comes before a fall.

Playing the maid

Never appear to seek power for its own sake.[7] During the hustings for election to leadership of the Conservative Party in 1990, candidates made it clear that their motives were for the good of the party, the good of the nation, pressure from colleagues to stand — anything but actually wanting to be Prime Minister.

Always try and make it look as if greatness is being thrust upon you. In Shakespeare's *Richard III*, the crowd beg the infamous usurper to accept the crown. Richard appears before them, dressed as a saintly cleric, more given to theology than secular affairs. The crowd are delighted and they press him all the more to accept. Richard, as he puts it, plays the maid, ie says 'No', but takes it.

Summary

- A diplomat is generally speaking, generally speaking.

- Diplomacy involves seeing situations for what they really are and people for what they really want.

- Diplomats give others what they want and say what they want to hear.

- It is not what you do that matters, but what you are seen to have done.

- It is important to understand the pressures that other people are under. Their problems are your problems.

- Try and see things as others see them.

- Attitude is a priceless asset. A positive attitude is much more powerful than a negative one.

- Always conduct yourself impeccably in public. Try and conceal negative feelings towards others.

- Keep your options open — always.

- Organizations are riddled with ambiguity and uncertainty; be prepared for all possibilities.

- When others try and obtain your support to further their own ends, respond with words like, 'maybe', 'someday', and 'when the time is right'.

- You have a right to change your mind.

- Avoid becoming caught in crossfire — divide and rule.

- Tact is making other people feel comfortable with you.

- It is better to say nothing than to criticize.

- If it is necessary to be negative, exercise restraint; eg point out the mistake and then blame yourself for it.

- A good model for delivering criticism is:
  - begin with two good things;
  - then deal with the bad things;
  - finish with another good thing.

- Think before you speak or act. Ask yourself, how might others see this? If in doubt, leave it out.

- If you say something tactless, retraction may only make matters worse.

- If you are as good as, or better than your boss, use your talents very carefully.

- You can win an argument with the boss, but only at the expense of losing the war.

- Really intelligent people are clever enough to appear stupid.

- Give others a stake in your achievements. Make them feel involved and successful too.

- Never flaunt success.

- Never appear to want power. Play the maid, ie say 'No', but take it.

DIPLOMACY QUESTIONNAIRE

Having read the chapter now re-test yourself:

1. **A colleague has just circulated a report which is a dreadful mess. He meets you on the corridor and asks what you think of it. What do you say?**

    a) 'Fine, excellent, just what we need.'
    b) 'It's awful.'
    c) 'Excellent, I have one or two tiny suggestions which you might be interested in.'
    d) 'I have not had time to read it yet.'

2. **You have forced an incompetent employee to resign. At the farewell dinner do you:**

    a) make a speech praising his work and regretting that his health prevented him from finishing it
    b) make a pleasant speech but without any reference to the employee's work
    c) omit the speeches
    d) develop a diplomatic illness and get someone else to make the presentation?

3. **A colleague is trying to form a breakaway department. He asks what your position would be if he were successful. What do you say?**

    a) you would definitely be interested in joining, and write a paper showing how your respective functions could be merged
    b) wish him well and say you would be interested in further discussion when the time is right
    c) you are happy as you are
    d) tell him he cannot succeed.

4. **You turned down a job offer a year ago because of a residency requirement, and have since regretted the decision. You then receive a telephone call asking if you are still interested in the job, which has unexpectedly become vacant again. What do you say?**

    a) 'Yes, I will accept on the terms previously offered.'
    b) 'I will accept only if the residency requirement is waived.'

c) 'What are you prepared to offer?'
d) 'I am willing to discuss it.'

5. **You are the owner of a dog kennel. One of your clients asks which is your favourite breed. Do you:**

    a) say 'I love all dogs' and then change the subject
    b) name your favourite breed
    c) name the client's favourite breed
    d) say 'I hate all dogs'.

6. **A less well qualified and experienced rival has beaten you to promotion. Do you:**

    a) lodge a grievance
    b) publicly doubt the other person's qualifications and capability
    c) send him a note of congratulations
    d) ask him for a job?

7. **A friend invites you to admire his new sports car. You have never seen anything so ugly. Do you say:**

    a) 'You paid how much for it?'
    b) 'It's a fine example of its kind.'
    c) 'I'm jealous.'
    d) 'I don't suppose you'd want to sell it to me?'

8. **You are looking for another job because you are tired of trying to operate with inadequate resources. What would you say to prospective employers?**

    a) be honest about your reason for wanting to leave
    b) say nothing unless asked, in which case, be honest about it
    c) explain that one of the things you like about your present job is the challenge of managing with minimal resources
    d) try and prevent your prospective employer from getting a word in edgeways.

9. **A new employee has just submitted a set of costings. They are nothing like what you wanted. Do you say:**

    a) 'This is quite good, it just needs tidying.'
    b) 'Obviously I did not make myself clear when I asked you to do this job.'
    c) 'This is complete rubbish.'
    d) 'You're sacked.'?

10. **You are convinced that one of your branch offices is over-staffed, but feel unable to exercise control from a distance. Would you:**

    a)   Involve the branch staff more in your own management meetings

    b)   transfer some of the staff to headquarters where you can supervise them

    c)   start holding management meetings at the branch

    d)   send in a work study team?

Answers opposite.

References

1. Goffman, E (1959) *The Presentation of Self in Everyday Life*, Doubleday Anchor, New York.
2. Schlenker, B R (1980) *Impression Management*, Brooks Cole, California.
3. Watzlawick, P, Weakland, J H, Fisch, R (1974) *Change: Principles of Problem Formation and Resolution*, Norton, New York.
4. Hackett, J (1983) *The Third World War: The Untold Story*, Sidgwick & Jackson, London.
5. Mortimer, P (1987) *Queen Elizabeth: A Life of the Queen Mother*, Penguin, Harmondsworth.
6. Hennested, B (1990) 'The symbolic impact of double bind leadership: Double bind and the dynamics of organization culture', *Journal of Management Studies*, 27(3), pp. 265–81.
7. Galbraith, J K (1984) *The Anatomy of Power*, Hamish Hamilton, London.

Answers to questionnaire

1. **d.**

2. **a.** He will believe you because he wants to believe you, and it is sensible to part with people on good terms and with generosity; you never know what may be round the next corner.

3. **b** — keep him dangling but keep your options open.

4. **d** — keep your options open.

5. **a.** Never reveal preferences. It offends many more people than it pleases.

6. **c.** Always behave impeccably in public. Try to conceal animosity, otherwise others will use it to divide and rule.

7. **b.**

8. **c** — be positive.

9. **b.**

10. **c** — enables you to observe without seeming to.

Score before reading chapter: ——

Score after reading chapter: ——

9

The power of reality

MANIPULATING REALITY QUESTIONNAIRE

Reality is a resource which can be used to make power. Test your ability to manipulate reality by answering the following quesions:

1. **An interviewer asks why you have never stayed longer than two years in any job. Do you reply:**

    a) 'I have yet to find a job I really like.'
    b) 'True, but I plan to stay here for at least five years.'
    c) 'I have always been willing to sacrifice personal comfort and security in order to take opportunities.'
    d) 'It's safer to be a moving target.'?

2. **A colleague in another department has ten support staff. Your department is three times the size and has 20 staff. Does that mean:**

    a) you are under-staffed
    b) the other department is over-staffed
    c) nothing, because the two departments are completely different
    d) the ratios are probably correct, given the different work undertaken by each department?

3. **What is your main problem at work?**

    a) not enough time
    b) too much pressure
    c) other departments
    d) your own inefficiency.

4. **You are extremely disturbed to learn that a particular**

contract is incurring huge losses. This could have serious implications for your career. Do you:

a) Prepare a CV and telephone a few employment agencies
b) say nothing and do nothing until you have seen the figures
c) say, 'That is what I would expect at this stage.'
d) angrily denounce the accounts office for their incompetence?

5. **Which of the following projects would you prefer to undertake?**

a) one where the groundwork is already complete
b) a totally new and exciting venture
c) a fairly interesting project involving collaboration with other departments
d) to rescue a venture which has run into difficulties.

6. **You are to chair a meeting concerning a merger between two departments. Would you:**

a) invite items for the agenda at the meeting
b) invite items for the agenda before the meeting
c) circulate an agenda before the meeting
d) circulate a brief paper outlining the options before the meeting?

7. **You have just had an uncomfortable discussion with your manager about your performance. Do you:**

a) try and forget about it as quickly as possible
b) make a note of the meeting
c) send him a note of the meeting
d) start looking for another job?

8. **After two months, you have succeeded in obtaining an appointment with a most senior manager to explain why you need more staff. Would you:**

a) write a short paper supplemented by a presentation
b) write a short paper and recite it
c) make a few notes before the start of the meeting
d) go, listen to what he says, and play it by ear?

9. **What is your policy on minuting meetings?**

a) a waste of time
b) you try and foist the task on to another department
c) you always write the minutes straight after the meeting
d) you write the minutes before the meeting?

10. **Your manager has just asked you to draft a new strategy and policy document for the department. Do you:**

   a) do nothing and hope he forgets about it
   b) scribble a few notes on two sheets of A4
   c) dictate a long rambling exposition full of buzz-words off the top of your head
   d) carry out careful research before compiling a well-thought, meticulous analysis?

Judge: Tell me, in your country what happens to a witness who does not tell the truth?

Witness: Begor, me Lord . . . his side usually wins.

> (Healy, M (1939) *The Old Munster Circuit*,
> Michael Joseph, London, p. 97)

Everything is real and nothing is real

Reality exists as individuals define it. King Lear's last words, 'Look there, look there,' for example, suggest that he may have died believing that his daughter Cordelia is still alive, when everyone else can see that she is dead.

Why is a gynaecological examination perceived as a clinical situation and not as a sexual encounter? Doctors are careful to define it as a purely clinical affair, but is it?

William Wallace, hero of the Scots, is often described by English historians as a thug and a cattle thief. Is that fair?

What is the truth? Reality often depends upon interpretation of facts. Facts, however, may lend themselves to more than one interpretation. Is the bottle half-full or half-empty? A first class honours degree from Cambridge, followed by a job in a merchant bank, is interpreted by most people as a successful career. To someone who wanted to be an actor, however, it is a tale of frustration and misery. Likewise, consider the two following statements:

Statement 1:

I come from a very poor background. We lived in a one-bedroom tenement block with no bath. It was a dank and gloomy hovel, the sitting room had only one tiny window. Is there any wonder then that I grew up nervous and depressed?

Statement 2:

I was born with a silver spoon in my mouth. The house I lived in as a child was modest, but we had a leading edge even then, being the only family in the block with an inside toilet.

These two statements are actually written by the same person and describe the same situation, yet they convey completely different impressions of the same objective conditions.

The elusive truth

Different people often have different perceptions of the truth. Consider, for example, the following 'facts':

1. Precise financial status of contract is unclear.

2. Believed to be running at a 25 per cent loss.

3. Productivity figures averaging only 80 psi instead of 112 psi; some gangs as low as 27 psi.

What is happening here? One interpretation is:

> The whole operation is a shambles. They have no idea where they are with the contract, which is just as well because the losses are probably through the roof. They've got gangs idle all over the place. In fact, from those productivity figures, it looks as if some of them are dead. We told them that the bonus scheme was unworkable when they set it up. They didn't listen, but just look at those productivity figures. They'll never achieve 112 psi, never.

Yet here is how another individual interpreted the same information:

> Having recently taken over an organization lacking even basic management information, it is encouraging to report that in a short space of time, work has progressed sufficiently to enable us to supply productivity data on the contract.
>
> These figures are of course likely to be qualified as the new procedures become fully operational. However, it is already evident that the financial position is not as bad as was initially feared. It is also clear that reservations about the viability of the new bonus scheme are unfounded. Certain sectors are already achieving more than 112 psi, which shows that productivity targets are attainable. Furthermore, our information systems are now sufficiently developed to monitor productivity. This is a remarkable achievement in such a short space of time, which now enables us to systematically investigate low-producing gangs, beginning with those most seriously below target. I am confident that the next report will show dramatic improvements.

Why reality matters

Child: Dad, is there really a monster in Loch Ness?

Father: Aye my wee pet; while ever tourists are spending their money, there'll always be a monster.

Reality is a resource which can be manipulated like any other. The aim of manipulation is:

to define reality to advantage.

The manager of a high-class restaurant, for example, was asked what he did when customers rejected a dish. After saying he never made a fuss, he added, 'A lot of people are too inexperienced to know what they are eating; that's the main reason food is sent back.' So plausible does this sound that few people ever question whether the food might actually be bad.

How to manipulate reality

Defining reality centres upon:

1. Awareness.

2. Detachment.

3. Control of information.

4. Influencing how information is interpreted.

5. Repetition.

Each of these is now discussed in turn.

Awareness: 'Give me the facts'

Power-seekers do not share the common faith in 'the facts', though they are adroit at manipulating such faith when they find it in others. Power-seekers know that:

there is no such thing as 'the facts.'

Different realities can be created according to how facts are:

- selected;
- emphasized;
- challenged.

As an exercise in point, imagine being asked to appear on the popular radio programme, *Desert Island Discs*. How would you like to be remembered: as brash and impatient; gentle, modest and kindly; or serious and intellectual? Any image is feasible, depending upon which questions you choose to answer; the emphasis devoted to different parts of the story, and the fact that a 45-minute programme offers little opportunity to challenge what is said.

In 1952 a 19-year-old educationally sub-normal youth called Derek Bentley was hanged for his part in the murder of a police constable. Bentley had not fired any shots, nor had he carried a gun. His conviction turned on the doctrine of joint responsibility, which in turn hinged largely upon Bentley's words, 'Let him have it.' The prosecution interpreted this as an incitement to shoot the police officer. The defence never suggested the alternative explanation, ie that Bentley was appealing to Craig to surrender his gun. While this extremely damaging 'fact' was emphasized, the equally significant fact that Bentley was under arrest when he spoke those words, and therefore no longer involved in the crime, was largely passed over. Further, the court never heard evidence about Bentley's medical condition, evidence which might have saved him from the gallows.[1] So much for facts.

Maintaining detachment

'Three o'clock: and all's well.'

Anyone exercising detachment and independent judgement possesses an edge, as they are less likely to be deceived by other people's definitions of reality. A few of the *Titanic*'s crew, for instance, realized that, given the position of the hole and the design of the ship, she must founder, despite the propaganda that 'God himself could not sink this ship'.[2]

Exercising detachment and independent judgement need not be difficult. Decision makers are typically reactive, blinkered, and drifting along.[3] They accept what they see and hear at face value, never realizing that reality is political.[4] If someone says there is a crisis, then a crisis exists. Conversely, if someone reports that all is well, then all is well.

Controlling information and interpretation of information

These two points are discussed together because of the overlap between them. The scope for manipulation is wide. It includes:

1. Defining the problem.

2. Defining the alternatives.[5]

3. Controlling the evaluation of alternatives.[6]

Defining the problem

It pays to be the one who defines the problem, as the way a problem is defined shapes subsequent action. Textbooks, for example, emphasize that 'the problem' of management is to motivate workers. Defining the issue in this way focuses attention on the workforce as 'the problem'. This detracts attention from managerial shortcomings. Inevitably then, poor productivity is attributed to a recalcitrant workforce. The latter's points about management's failure to provide adequate equipment, balance the work-flow, and so on, are dismissed as mere grumbling.[7,8]

Likewise, a candidate for a job in a personnel office once said, 'I suppose the unions are the main problem.' The personnel manager replied, 'The unions are not my problem. My problem is the management.' On hearing this, the candidate concluded, 'This man knows nothing about industrial relations.' In fact, the reverse was true. The personnel manager understood the importance of identifying the right problem. Since his job was to manage the trade unions, defining management as 'the problem' enabled him to divert attention from his own performance by leading others to assume that relations with the trade unions were good. Furthermore, any rupture could be attributed to management.

'My problem is'

Sound advice for power-seekers is:

> *identify only with problems you can solve.*

Better still,

> *identify only with problems you have already solved.*

Why take the ills of the organization upon your shoulders by making extravagant promises? If no one else can cure them, the probability is that neither can you. For example, if the organization's basic marketing strategy is wrong, then no new product, however brilliant, is going to rescue it. Promise a new product by all means, but be circumspect about the expectations you raise.

The best challenges to accept are those which you have already accomplished. 'I will produce a drawing by Friday,' says the architect.

His boss is impressed, and even more so when, on Friday, the drawing appears. What he did not know, however, was that the drawing had been in the architect's desk for six months.

An even better power ploy is to:

create a crisis and then solve it.

Declare an emergency; cancel leave and convene urgent meetings to discuss the situation. Ensure lights burn late, pull people in on Saturdays for further emergency meetings. Let words like 'redundancy' and 'collapse' hang in the air as people wait in corridors anxious for any news or decision. Issue bulletins, make 'backs-to-the-wall' speeches, gravely address mass gatherings of staff, and so on. This requires courage to enact, but the results are spectacular.[9]

'Your problem is'

Be careful how others define your problems. They will foist hopeless cases on to you if they can, and seek to exploit your weaknesses. For instance, a new graduate employee is told that his problem is to operate an efficient delivery service. He is being set up to fail, as the fleet is over ten years' old, yet he bravely struggles with the problem.

One way of countering is to blame problems upon exogenous factors such as other departments, changes in government policy, supply failures and the like. The problem with this tactic, however, is that it can sound like making excuses, especially if used frequently. It is therefore better to try and redefine the problem. For example:

Ten ways to begin redefining a problem

1. 'That is not the issue: what we need to concern ourselves with is . . . .'

2. 'Let's not go looking for problems where there are none.'

3. 'I see no conflict between the two objectives. My problem is . . . .'

4. 'I wish that was the problem.'

5. 'X is not my problem. My problem is . . . .'

6. 'That is the least of my worries.'

7. 'If that is the worst thing that happens to us, we will have done well.'

8. 'X isn't important, what matters is . . . .'

9. 'I agree that is a concern. However, a much bigger problem is . . . .'

10. 'X is a thorn in our side, not a dagger in the heart.'

Who owns the problem?

A problem shared is a problem dumped. Help someone with a problem, and before you know where you are, it becomes your problem and the reality is that you are responsible for it. Make sure others understand your role, and be seen to fulfil it. The surest means of doing so is to commit your advice to writing. Take, for example, this memorandum from the city catering officer to the director of museums concerning the latter's proposal to create a high-class museum restaurant.

> My advice is that the proposal has no prospect of succeeding. The number of visitors to the museum is too small to make a restaurant viable, and there is no passing trade to boost custom. I cannot see, therefore, any justification for investment.

Despite this advice, the proposal was implemented. By the end of the first year, losses totalled £160,000. Had it not been for that memorandum, the museum management might have claimed that they were ill-advised by the catering department, or not advised at all.

Resist the temptation to do other people's job for them, whatever sort of mess they may be making of it. Having foisted responsibility on to you, the other person will then complain 'It was all taken out of my hands.'

Controlling alternatives

Defining the alternatives

If it is too late to define the problem, the next best thing is to control the solution. Choice of solution depends upon the alternatives considered. Power-seekers therefore aim to limit the agenda according to what suits their purpose.

This is usually fairly easy. All that you need do is declare 'there are two alternatives', or 'the alternatives are . . . .' Once the alternatives are established it is very difficult for an opponent to extend the list, as decision makers lack the time and the mental capacity to cope with more than a few options.[10] Anything requiring further expenditure of effort is likely to be rejected. The probability of rejection increases with time.

The best way of controlling the agenda is to set out the alternatives in writing, such as a position paper or a policy document. Not only does this capture attention, but any verbal counter-arguments fade into the ether as your document proceeds to the next stage of the decision making process.

Controlling information about alternatives

Controlling information about alternatives is another means of influencing outcomes. The commonest ploys are:[11]

- 'It won't work';
- 'X [person or body] will not approve',

closely followed by:

- 'We don't have the resources';
- 'Option X has the support of . . .'.

Suppression often succeeds simply because since such statements seem highly plausible, no one bothers to investigate.

Another possibility is to manipulate factual information about alternatives — for example, emphasizing the reliability of a particular product when it is known that reliability is a critical factor determining choice. Tailoring application forms to match job requirements is another example of this technique. The curriculum vitae contains the full information; the letter of application stresses some facts while ignoring others.

The power of repetition

Sometimes, we know things only because we have heard them so often that we assume they are true. We believe, for example, that butchers' animals are slaughtered humanely. Evidence from the meat and poultry industry, however, is that:

> It is generally acknowledged that the most 'humane' method of stunning is the captive bolt pistol . . . . It is a horrifying fact that most of the cattle shot in this way are not stunned but stand grievously wounded and fully conscious while the pistol is reloaded. Even when the shot is more accurate, slaughtermen acknowledge the difficulty of knowing when an animal is properly stunned.
> Poultry fare no better . . . . Many birds (moving towards their

deaths hung upside down on a moving conveyor belt) were inefficiently stunned, so that 'a substantial number may still be sensitive' when slaughtered. This . . . results in 'some birds entering the scalding tank before they are dead'.

(Gold, M (1988) *Living Without Cruelty*, Greenprint, Basingstoke, p.12.)

Reality is created by repeating the same message over and over again, regardless of whether it is true or false. The longer and more frequently a message is heard, the more deeply embedded it becomes. The message for power-seekers is simple, ie keep telling people whatever it is you want them to believe.

Once others have absorbed the message, make it look as if it is they who are saying it, and not you. For example, 'You are right, we do have a lot of expertise in that area', and, 'As you say, we are a caring organization.' Eventually transferal occurs, ie the other person internalizes your opinion as their own.[12, 13]

Repetition is also an effective response to challenge. Although it can be tedious to say the same thing over and over again, it is extremely effective because it prevents the other party from scoring a point or gaining a concession. The most difficult court witness to cross-examine, for example, is the one who keeps giving the same reply to questions, such as, 'My answer is set out in my report.' Conversely, the witness who tries to explain or embellish a point often becomes tied in knots.

Countering other people's attempts to define reality

Exposing assumptions

Power derives from unchallenged assumptions.[14, 15] The most penetrating question in this context, therefore is:

how do you know?

Exposing assumptions requires an enquiring mind and persistence. Senior managers, for example, once told the organization's equality officer that the trade unions were 'dead against' job-sharing. The equality officer decided to probe, however. Consequently, he learned that the trade unions were indeed opposed to job-sharing, and not interested in negotiating an agreement on the topic. However, if any of their members wished to job-share, that was their business.

This was quite different of course from saying that no manual worker must be allowed to job-share. Management here had used a partial truth to create a reality which suited them, as they disliked the equality officer and took every opportunity to thwart him. The equality officer's challenge revealed a small but significant difference between fact and assumption.

To take another example, which also concerns equal opportunities, a dispute arose over the employment of Muslims in school kitchens. Catering managers, who resented the intervention of race equality officers, said that employment of Muslims was impossible because kitchen staff were required under their conditions of service to carry out all food-preparation tasks. Since this included handling pork, Muslims were effectively debarred from employment.

The race equality officer quietly consulted the Conditions of Service handbook. He found that this document merely listed the broad duties of the various grades of kitchen staff, such as washing up, observance of hygiene regulations and assisting with serving meals. The only reference to cooking was 'To assist with the preparation of food.' So, despite what the catering managers were leading everyone to believe, no clear and definite rule existed whereby staff were required to handle pork.

The catering managers then argued that by custom and practice, the clause 'To assist with the preparation of food' required staff to carry out all associated duties. Moreover, the catering managers enlisted the support of the trade unions, as all attention focused upon the principle of 'no exception'. After all, it was argued, the same conditions of service required all staff to handle halal meat. Would they be allowed to decline to perform this task on grounds of conscience? Perhaps, suggested the catering managers rhetorically, the solution was to delete pork, the cheapest form of animal protein, from school dinner menus?

The purpose of these arguments was to keep the debate focused upon the issue of exemption, knowing that this problem was unresolvable. In other words, it was the assumptions about the problem, rather than the problem itself, that impeded the solution. While ever people believed that Muslim leaders would demand exemption from handling pork, the catering managers had power. In fact, as the race equality officer discovered, Muslims *were* prepared to handle pork, provided they wore gloves.

In practice, Muslim staff tended to work with halal meat, and indigenous staff with non-halal meat. It was, and still is, a perfectly harmonious if informal arrangement, which shows that the exemption argument, too, was nonsense. What is interesting, though, was its almost unquestioned acceptance.

Wood bends: how to do things with rules

People often find it convenient to hide behind rules. Typically, the argument is that rules are rules, and even if they are bad rules, they must be followed until such time as they are amended. This is a good argument if the rules happen to serve your purpose. If not, change reality by arguing that the rules are:

- counter-productive to efficacy; or
- result in unfairness; and therefore

it is a nonsense to uphold them.

Deal firmly with rule-bound bureaucrats. Remember:

your argument is better than theirs.

Secondly:

if necessary, appeal to a higher level.

If a rule is nonsensical, then logically your argument must be stronger because it is sensible and just. By all means try and convince the other party, but be prepared to go over his head. Never advertise your intentions, however, or the other person will forestall you. Allowing them to be heard first makes your task more difficult. Ignore counter-arguments about the difficulties of changing rules. Few organizational ordinances are set in stone:

> An education authority faced a problem when a school governing body chose to issue a Written Warning to a headteacher. The education authority strongly felt that the case warranted dismissal but they were helpless as under the school's Articles of Government, the governors' decision was final. Everyone was at a loss until a bright personnel officer [not the author] found that the Education Act 1944 vested ultimate responsibility for education with the local authority. This, he argued, must imply that the local authority has ultimate power. The High Court agreed; an Act of Parliament takes precedence over local Articles of Government.

How to handle meetings

Prepare ye the way

To get what you want, the essential prerequisite is:

to know what you want.

This is not as obvious as it sounds. People often attend even the most critically important meetings without clear objectives or plan, guided only by vague hope and intuition. Afterwards, they wonder why they have done badly. Power-seekers see meetings as opportunities. They know that:

preparation is power.

Preparation involves identifying objectives and a game plan. This need not be complex or time-consuming, though it is a good idea to jot down the fruits of your deliberations. For example:

1. What are my objectives?

2. What support/obstacles can I expect?

3. What questions should I ask?

4. How might I pursue this if I succeed?

5. If I fail, or the cost seems too high, what other options do I possess?

Even a simple informal plan such as this is a powerful weapon, especially when ranged against the unready.

Capturing the floor

The importance of preparing some form of paper was mentioned earlier in this chapter. Supplementing such a document with a presentation further increases the likelihood of success, by enabling the presenter to define reality to advantage. Specifically, a presentation:

1. Arrests attention.

2. Minimizes interruptions.

3. Facilitates understanding.

4. Enables the presenter to concentrate upon favourable data.

People enjoy being entertained. They would far rather listen to a lively presentation than work through pages of dry statistical information. Presentations normally prevent others from interrupting or engaging in other blocking behaviour such as changing the subject, cracking jokes and arguing. Since a presentation increases the chance of being heard, it also enhances the probability of being understood. This is important, as the most common reason for rejecting ideas is not some Machiavellian conspiracy, but because people simply do not understand them.

The presenter controls the delivery. This enables more favourable information to be emphasized, and vice versa. Experience suggests that the most common reason for rejection of ideas is the recipients' failure to understand them. A presentation substantially reduces that risk. Research indicates that a good presentation carries more weight than documentary evidence, however sound the latter.[16] A good presentation is one which:[17]

1. Stimulates and communicates vision through the use of anecdotes, pictures and other vivid material.

2. Creates an attractive picture of the future and keeps the audience's attention firmly fixed upon it.

3. Appeals to the decision maker's prejudices.

4. Makes the decision maker feel infallible, by providing evidence of success, recalling the decision maker's previous successes, and making the decision maker feel in control.[18, 19]

Evidence exists which suggests that this technique works even when the information conveyed by the presenter and objective statistical data clearly contradict each other. It works because the latter tend to be ignored — think of the scope this provides power-seekers with!

Minutes first, meeting later

The old adage 'He who writes the minutes has power', is well-founded. Power emanates from the scope to manipulate:

1. The atmosphere of the discussion.

2. The arguments expressed.

3. The decisions.

Even where a rigid style of minuting is *de rigueur*, room for manoeuvre always exists. For example, decisions are often vague, thus enabling the minute-writer to exercise discretion in deciding how to word them.

Minutes, incidentally, are legally admissible documents. The sooner after the meeting they are written, the better. For that reason, it is advisable to indicate the date at which they were written up on the paper. A very powerful approach is to write the minutes *before* the meeting. This is actually quite easy and extremely productive, as it forces clear thinking about objectives and helps guide the discussion accordingly.

Getting it in writing

It is emphasized that:

a document is many times more powerful than the spoken word.

This is because documentation serves to:

- focus attention;
- stimulate a response;
- create reality.

Even simple matters such as transfer requests, instructions and complaints, possess more force when committed to writing. Written communications demand a response and can therefore serve to galvanize the other party into action. Moreover, since they can be worded so as to require a reply, they can be used to force someone to commit themselves in writing.

CYA

Written records are an excellent defensive tactic, known to the streetwise as CYA (Cover Your Arse). The doctor who can show from his records, for example, that he injected a given quantity of a drug into a patient at a given time is in a much stronger position than one who vaguely remembers that he 'must have done'. This applies even where the former is lying and the latter is doing his best to recollect the truth. Cynical though it may sound, what matters is:

not what you do;

but,

what you can prove you have done.

Whenever a major disaster occurs, for example, even as the dead are being recovered from the wreckage, behind the scenes, filing cabinets are being ransacked. The health and safety officer, for instance, is suddenly desperate to find copy letters proving that he had warned that fire precautions were inadequate.

Attack is always the best method of defence. For example:

> Mr X came to see me on Thursday afternoon. After a long and incoherent statement by Mr X it eventually emerged that the purpose of his visit to my office was to enquire what I intended to do about his appeal against his examination results. I said that as he had chosen to go straight to the Principal without discussing his concerns with me as Course Tutor, I intended to do nothing. Mr X then made some derogatory remarks about the academic staff of the department by which I understood him to mean that he felt that his examination papers had been marked unfairly and that he had been discriminated against because of his race.
>
> I am extremely concerned about this student's high-handed and irresponsible behaviour. It is unacceptable to me that he should continue to make slanderous allegations about the integrity and professionalism of my staff. If Mr X continues to behave in this way, he can expect only such consideration and assistance as he is formally entitled to.

In fact, the student had been treated unfairly, as the course tutor knew. The self-righteous tone of this onslaught, however, makes the student appear as a trouble-maker.

Playing to the gallery

Power-seekers are always on the look-out for opportunities to present themselves in a good light. Take this honeyed communication, for instance:

> I acknowledge receipt of your letter of resignation which I reluctantly accept. I am aware that over the last eighteen months, the job of centre manager has become extremely unrewarding and I understand and empathize with your reasons for wishing to develop your career in a new direction. I thank you most sincerely for your sustained contribution, and wish you well in your new job. Please keep in touch with us.

The goodwill expressed in this letter hardly suggests that the employee resigned because he felt his manager had ceased to take an interest in his work. Instead, the author creates an impression of himself as a pleasant and considerate supervisor, knowing that the letter will be copied to the personnel department and his senior colleagues.

Documents should always be composed with the future in mind. A memorandum to an employee expressing concern about his performance is written not so much for the employee's benefit, but to enable the writer to prove, perhaps ultimately to an industrial tribunal, that he has behaved reasonably. For example:

> I refer to our discussion this morning concerning the new staffing proposals for the engineering workshop. I said that I was concerned as these should have been finished eighteen months ago. However, despite several assurances from you over the past six months, they have not yet been produced in a satisfactory form.
>
> You said that you felt upset because your proposals had twice been rejected. I explained that this was because they contained no reasoning or strategy for change. You said that you were doing your best but could not understand what was wanted. We agreed therefore that you would transfer to my office temporarily and produce the proposals with my direct assistance.

This memorandum is only partially accurate. The employee is indeed barely competent, but, what is under-emphasized, however, is that the manager's vague briefing is making the problem worse. The document envisages the following report to senior management:

> We've been waiting more than eighteen months for that restructure. I've sent it back twice because it was rubbish. He said he didn't understand what was wanted so I even had him down in my office, held his hand and he still can't do it.

In other words, 'Look what a good manager I am. I have counselled the employee. I have made my concerns clear. I have given him special support and attention. What more can I do?'

The last word wins

Power-seekers need to recognize when CYA tactics are being used against them. The essential point to remember is:

the last word usually wins.

Take this seemingly routine communication, for instance:

Please would you note that the following exhibition dates:

The background to this memorandum is that the previous year, the exhibition had been a shambles. Materials had arrived late, dates had been forgotten, the wrong exhibits were delivered, and so forth. The publicity manager blamed the administrator, and vice versa. This note is the publicity manager's insurance against a repeat of the previous year's problems. That is, he can say 'I gave Jim a list of dates well in advance. Here it is, see for yourself. No excuse.' Jim, however, was match for the publicity manager:

> Thank you for the list of exhibition dates which I have now entered in my diary. Please could you ensure that I have full details, supplies and materials at least 14 days before each event.

Jim wins by turning the tables, and by ensuring that his is that last communication on the subject. The onus is now upon the publicity manager to discharge his obligations.

Likewise:

> *Mike*
> I am away for the rest of this week. Since I have not heard from you, I assume that you have not been able to obtain confirmation of the price and therefore the order is cancelled.
> *Bill*

Securing the last word here absolves Bill from further responsibility. If the order is subsequently processed and a loss ensues, Mike cannot blame Bill, nor can anyone suggest that Bill was guilty of allowing a breakdown in communications.

Wars of words

If your opponent is cognizant of CYA tactics a war may develop, as each party tries to secure the last word through memorandum and counter-memorandum. If this happens, take the initiative and:

> *go and see the other person.*

This does not always work, but it does at least give the protagonists a chance to develop a better understanding of one another and maybe convert a negative relationship into a positive one.

Grasping the initiative

Never wait to be asked to produce a document or confirm matters in writing, just do it. Do not be deterred by the possibility of causing upset. Provided the communication is respectful, that is sufficient. Where meetings are concerned, the chairperson will probably be glad that someone has done the work.

Never an angry or fanciful word

Documents are more difficult to retract or deny than the spoken word. They are potentially double-edged and should therefore be composed with the utmost care, and never be influenced by anger or elation.[20] By all means write a letter telling someone what you think of them, but do not post it. Likewise, by all means draft a proposal brimming with enthusiasm and promises, but do not circulate that either. It is advisable to leave any important composition for a few days, or at least overnight, before finalizing it. It is surprising what improvements suggest themselves, and how an angry or enthusiastic statement, which seemed apposite the previous evening, on second thoughts is clearly an over-reaction. Let all composition be guided by the lawyer's mottos ie:[21]

1. Think how it would sound read out in court.

2. If in doubt, leave it out.

From ghosts and shadows

Seeing is believing, whatever the reality. Truth is what others believe or can be led to believe. Power-seekers know this, and that:

working smart often achieves more than working hard.

Again, it is not what you do that counts, but what you are seen to have done. Written evidence, especially when copious, seldom fails to impress, regardless of what actually lies behind it. For example, a new director was enthusiastic about implementing an establishment review. Before going on holiday, he instructed that plans should be well advanced by his return, as indeed they were. On his desk was a ten-page report packed with analyses, charts and diagrams. Extracts of the document are quoted below:

> This report and the recommendations it contains are the product of extensive and detailed discussion with the client division. We broadly concur on all the major issues but feel it would be useful to talk over some points of detail with you.
> Essentially, the underlying philosophy of our approach is that all directly operational divisions should be part of the same manage-

ment structure. We simultaneously recognize the need for a strong client department sufficiently large to remain independently viable . . . .

One of the exciting managerial challenges identified as a result of our analysis has been . . .

The director was extremely gratified to learn that his instructions had prompted 'extensive and detailed discussions': clearly a great deal of intense activity had taken place in his absence. He was further pleased by the evidence of good working relations between members of his management team suggested by the phrase 'We broadly concur'. His subordinates are careful, however, to show that they still need him as counsellor and advisor to 'talk over' issues they have been unable to resolve. The phrase 'exciting managerial challenges' suggests a positive attitude on the part of the subordinates, while the word 'analysis' conveys the impression of a systematic and exacting approach.

The director might have been less impressed, however, had he been aware of the conversation between the managers of the two divisions which led to the production of the report:

MANAGER A: God knows what he wants this for. We've just had a restructure.

MANAGER B: Well I think we have to keep him happy. It seems to me the big issue is whether we transfer the workshops from your division into mine or leave them where they are. It makes sense to transfer them but I don't particularly want them.

MANAGER A: I don't blame you. My problem is I have a load of staff doing nothing, but what can you do when they won't let us make anyone redundant?

MANAGER B: It's not just that. You and I know this review isn't going anywhere anyway. Central Personnel have said they aren't interested. It's only a year since the last review was implemented. If we spend hours on it, it's all going to be a waste of time.

MANAGER A: True. So what do you want to do?

MANAGER B: Well he said he wanted us to consult and work it out, so tell you what, I'll knock something together, you take a look at it and hopefully, that's the last we'll hear of it.

Sometimes success can be achieved with no effort at all. For example:

> The trade unions of a small engineering workshop were due to discuss the annual pay award with the manager. The manager, who had authority to pay up to 8 per cent, greeted the trade unions politely but gravely. Trading conditions, he explained, were difficult. Consequently his instructions were that 2.5 per cent was the limit. As he made this offer, he looked embarrassed. Eventually he said, 'Look, I feel terrible about offering you this. I am going down to head office and I'm not leaving till they come up with something better.'
>
> The manager then booked a day's leave but asked his secretary to make it known that he was in London. The trade unions waited pensively. When the manager returned, he said: 'That was some struggle. They would not budge. In fact they even talked about withdrawing the two-and-a-half per cent. After about two hours they suggested three-and-a-half per cent. I told them I wasn't going to insult you lads with that sort of figure. If that was the best they could do, they could come and negotiate it themselves. Anyway, you'll be pleased to know that in the end, I got them to double their offer to five per cent.'

The trade unions were delighted. Here was a manager willing to fight for his staff, a rare quality indeed!

Reality, then, is a curious phenomenon. Organizational life is sometimes akin to Samuel Becket's play, *Waiting for Godot*. The plot concerns two tramps waiting for a man called Godot. By the time the play finishes, no one is any the wiser as to who Godot is; why the two tramps are waiting for him, whether he will ever come at all, or, whether he has come and gone unnoticed.

Summary

- Reality exists as individuals define it.
- Reality often depends upon interpretation of facts.
- Facts, however, can be interpreted differently.
- Power-seekers aim to define reality to their advantage
- There is no such thing as 'the facts'.
- Maintain independent judgement, and act upon it.
- Controlling the way a problem is defined is an important source of power, because it determines subsequent action.

- Identify only with problems that are resolvable, or, better still, with problems you have already resolved.

- Be wary of how others try and define your problems.

- A problem shared is a problem dumped.

- If the problem-definition cannot be controlled, try and control the options considered. Failing that, seek control over information about the options.

- Repetition is a powerful means of creating reality.

- Power derives from assumptions. Exposing assumptions requires an enquiring mind and persistence.

- Rules are only rules if they suit you. If not, argue that the rules are a nonsense and must be changed.

- To get what you want, the first essential is to know what you want, and then to prepare accordingly.

- Discussion documents, presentations etc can be used to get what you want.

- A lively and vivid presentation can induce people to disregard unfavourable statistical data.

- He who writes the minutes has power, especially if he writes them before the meeting.

- A document is many times more powerful than the spoken word.

- What matters is not what you have done, but what you can prove you have done.

- Documents can be used to create a favourable impression of the writer.

- He who has the last word usually wins.

- Never wait to be asked to produce a document, just do it.

- Never despatch a document written in anger or elation.

- 'From ghosts and shadows to the truth': the power-seeker's truth.

MANIPULATING REALITY QUESTIONNAIRE

Having read the chapter, now re-test yourself.

1. **An interviewer asks why you have never stayed in a job longer than two years. Do you reply:**
   a) 'I have yet to find a job I really like.'
   b) 'True, but I plan to stay here for at least five years.'
   c) 'I have always been willing to sacrifice personal comfort and security in order to take opportunities.'
   d) 'It's safer to be a moving target.'?

2. **A colleague in another department has ten support staff. Your department is three times the size and has 20 staff. Does that mean:**
   a) you are under-staffed
   b) the other department is over-staffed
   c) nothing, because the two departments are completely different
   d) the ratios are probably correct, given the different work undertaken by each department?

3. **What is your main problem at work?**
   a) not enough time
   b) too much pressure
   c) other departments
   d) your own inefficiency.

4. **You are extremely disturbed to learn that a particular contract is incurring huge losses. This could have serious implications for your career. Do you:**
   a) prepare a CV and telephone a few employment agencies
   b) say nothing and do nothing until you have seen the figures
   c) say, 'That is what I would expect at this stage.'
   d) angrily denounce the accounts office for their incompetence?

5. **Which of the following projects would you prefer to undertake?**
   a) one where the groundwork is already complete
   b) a totally new and exciting venture

c) a fairly interesting project involving collaboration with other departments
d) to rescue a venture which has run into difficulties.

6. **You are to chair a meeting concerning a merger between two departments. Would you:**

a) invite items for the agenda at the meeting
b) invite items for the agenda before the meeting
c) circulate an agenda before the meeting
d) circulate a brief paper outlining the options before the meeting?

7. **You have just had an uncomfortable discussion with your manager about your performance. Do you:**

a) try and forget about it as quickly as possible
b) make a note of the meeting
c) send him a note of the meeting
d) start looking for another job?

8. **After two months, you have succeeded in obtaining an appointment with a most senior manager to explain why you need more staff. Would you:**

a) write a short paper supplemented by a presentation
b) write a short paper and recite it
c) make a few notes before the start of the meeting
d) go, listen to what he says, and play it by ear?

9. **What is your policy on minuting meetings?**

a) a waste of time
b) you try and foist the task on to another department
c) you always write the minutes straight after the meeting
d) you write the minutes before the meeting?

10. **Your manager has just asked you to draft a new strategy and policy document for the department. Do you:**

a) do nothing and hope he forgets about it
b) scribble a few notes on two sheets of A4
c) dictate a long rambling exposition full of buzz-words off the top of your head
d) carry out careful research before compiling a well thought, meticulous analysis?

Answers overleaf.

References

1. Yallop, D (1990) *To Encourage the Others*, Corgi, London.
2. Lord, W A (1976) *A Night To Remember*, Penguin, Harmondsworth.
3. Lindblom, C E 'The science of muddling through', *Public Administration Review*, 1959, XIX(2), pp.79–88.
4. Stephenson, T (1985) *Management: A Political Activity*, Macmillan, London.
5. Pfeffer, J (1981) *Power in Organizations*, Pitman, Boston.
6. Pfeffer, op. cit.
7. Crosby, P (1979) *Quality is Free*, McGraw-Hill, New York.
8. Deming, E (1982) *Out of the Crisis*, Cambridge University Press, Cambridge.
9. Korda, M (1976) *Power*, Ballantine Books, New York.
10. Simon, H A (1960) *The New Science of Management Decision*, Harper, New York.
11. Bacharach, P and Baratz, M S (1970) *Power and Poverty: Theory and Practice*, Oxford University Press, New York.
12. Kelman, H C (1958) 'Compliance, identification and internalization, three processes of attitude change', *Journal of Conflict Resolution*, 11(1), pp. 51–60.
13. Kanter, R M (1968) 'Commitment and social organization: A study of commitment mechanisms in utopian communities', *American Sociological Review*, 33, pp. 499–517.
14. Lukes, S (1974) *Power: A Radical View*, Macmillan, London.
15. Martin, R (1977) *The Sociology of Power*, Routledge & Kegan Paul, London.
16. Schwenk, C R (1986) 'Information, cognitive biases and commitment to a course of action', *Academy of Management Review*, 11(2), pp. 290–310.
17. See Drummond, H (1991) *Effective Decision Making: A Practical Guide for Management*, Kogan Page, London, for a fuller description of this technique.
18. Taylor, S and Thompson, S (1982) 'Stalking the elusive "vividness" effect', *Psychological Review*, 89, pp. 155–81.
19. Langer, E J (1983) *The Psychology of Control*, Sage, Beverly Hills.
20. Janis, I L (1989) *Crucial Decisions: Leadership in Policy Making and Crisis Management*, Free Press, New York.
21. Napley, D (1975) *The Technique of Persuasion*, Sweet & Maxwell, London.

Answers to questionnaire

1. **c** — always give a positive impression.

2. **a** — you may as well interpret the facts to suit you.

3. **c** — why make yourself look weak or incompetent?

4. **c** enables you to keep the initiative while you investigate. D is a possibility but at the expense of drawing attention to the problem.

5. **a** — stick to problems you know you can solve.

6. **d**.

7. **c** — and fast, before he beats you to it.

8. **a**. D is hopeless — if you let the other party take the initiative they will use it to deliver a sermon about the need for cost cutting, and so on. After that you can forget any hope of obtaining more staff.

9. **d** — always.

10. **c** — give him what he wants to see, but do not waste time over it as such documents are usually skimmed rather than read, and rarely go further than the filing cabinet.

Score before reading chapter ——

Score after reading chapter   ——

Index